"There is risk in stepping across the chasm between the status quo and a new way."

Leading the Way

*New ideas, new ways,
new people to face challenges*

There's a definition of leadership I've always liked. It posits that leadership is the ability to persuade people to go where they don't necessarily want to go.

Picture a scene from World War II: Allied soldiers are fighting their way across Europe, and a platoon is pinned down under enemy fire. The sergeant knows the men would be safer and more likely to drive the enemy back if they can get to the next knoll. But bullets are flying through the air between where the platoon is hunkered down and that knoll.

Getting those men to sprint across that life-threatening gulf is leadership.

Sometimes, it's demonstrating that it can be done. So maybe the sergeant runs across first. Other times, it's describing the benefits that await those who cross. That means explaining the plan in a way that persuades the troops to move, out of self-interest. Still other times, leadership means cashing in on the loyalty the sergeant has earned over the course of the campaign, making the case that his recommendations usually prove correct.

Life on our islands is nothing like the horrors of war, but the same principles apply. Moving into new ways of doing things, with a younger generation getting involved, and relying on people who perhaps have not lived here long, can be frightening. And there certainly is risk in stepping across the chasm between the status quo and a new way.

But there also is risk in not addressing our challenges.

Maine senator Angus King, during his years as governor, would welcome schoolchildren on tours of the state house, and point to the state seal, with the Latin phrase, *Dirigo*, which means "I lead." King would ask the kids if they knew what the word meant, and when they didn't, he would tell them—tongue in cheek—that it meant, "We've never tried it that way before."

Too often, King correctly implied, that's the response to new ideas.

In this edition of *Island Journal*, we explore the theme of leadership. As readers may know, the Island Institute works to help community leaders take on the challenges of their island and remote coastal communities. Our I-LEAD program focuses on helping nonprofits better serve their constituents, and our economic development work and Island and Coastal Innovation Fund (ICIF) give business leaders support as they expand services, like those provided by island stores and fuel delivery businesses.

Our story offerings include a look at aquaculture as an emerging economic sector that may supplement or even replace lobster fishing for some. Another story examines solutions to the moral imperative of allowing our elderly islanders to live their last years close to home, near their family and friends. We also tell the story of a younger man who saw the high prices Casco Bay islanders were paying for heating fuel and decided to start a business that would lower those costs.

And another story recounts how Vinalhaven hired a man in his 20s as town manager, and decided to invest in his education.

Of course, this being *Island Journal*, we've gathered plenty more island-specific stories and photos we hope capture the unique and wonderful quality of life here. Hope you enjoy!

—Tom Groening, editor

ISLAND JOURNAL

Celebrating Island Life & Culture

Volume 32

*Looking out to the Cranberry Isles
from the top of Cadillac Mountain in
Acadia National Park*
ERIC WAYNE

Leadership in the Age of Ambiguity

Maine Maritime Academy, College of the Atlantic, Island Institute presidents talk elements of leadership

They represent three very different organizations, but in many ways, College of the Atlantic (COA) in Bar Harbor, Maine Maritime Academy (MMA) in Castine, and the Island Institute, based in Rockland, each have an oar in the water and are pulling together in making coastal Maine and the islands places where communities and the economy function and thrive.

Each organization's president—Darron Collins of COA, Bill Brennan of MMA, and the Island Institute's Rob Snyder—gathered on the MMA campus earlier this year and engaged in a wide-ranging discussion about the region's future.

IJ: Leadership is a theme we're exploring in this year's *Island Journal*, and it can be examined from very different perspectives, some of which are represented by the three organizations here.

Snyder: There's this big question: Where's the future of leadership going to come from? And what's the future of civic leadership look like? And that's why I was really interested in talking with you guys, because when you think about civic leadership, you're thinking about one set of values—how we build more cohesive, collaborative communities that can deal with change. And on the other hand, how do we think competitively enough to build the next economy that's going to add to—if we're lucky—the lobster industry's success. What does the next ocean economy look like?

What I'm really struggling with is, how do we work together to move young people into [fulfilling] these needs we have as the older generation ages out? And how do we, as organizations, feed the creation of that next generation?

Brennan: The points that you're raising are issues that I saw 30 years ago when I was Marine Resources commissioner. I spent all my time traveling up and down the coast, and I was counting on the civic leadership that existed in those communities, because it was important to what I was trying to do.

I was advocating for a devolution of our management authority, to get it away from this state-centric model. And I used examples that I'd grown up with here in Castine, going to town meetings and seeing local people. Why is the government, as represented by Augusta, the only place decisions can be made? Every one of these communities has people who come together at town meeting time, and they make decisions on how they're going to spend their money.

One of the issues we have here is trying to convince a kid in, say, Deer Isle—who's getting ready to get out of high school and trying to make a decision about whether to go to college, and he knows he can make a lot of money continuing to fish, and yet, I know how hard that life is—to pursue further educational opportunities.

One of my former marine patrol officers, who was from a fishing community, when I got here as president, his kid was a junior, and he graduated and went to sea and made a lot of money. He just joined us on the training cruise as a licensed officer. But he's back fishing. He developed the opportunity to do what he was raised doing, what he knew in his own community, but we provided him with an opportunity to enhance his options. And he certainly brings to bear, in his community, the leadership skills that he developed here.

IJ: Let's talk about these young people. The class that starts college in September, at both your institutions, will have been born at the start of the 21st century. What's different about this generation? What values will they need to lead in their fields?

Collins: I went to COA. I started in '88 and graduated in '92, which was right after the college had survived a devastating fire. The generation that came before me were the real pioneers. They came when we weren't accredited, and they were transferring from the Ivys and the elite liberal arts institutions. There was a real demand for an alternative approach to education, especially on the coast of Maine.

I think the incoming class has to be able to deal with ambiguity, which I think is an interesting leadership characteristic. The world is a really complex place. There are very few black-and-white answers. Helping our own students become comfortable in this ambiguity is really important.

Leadership is a pretty broad term and can mean a lot of different things. What we do with our students is present them with a great balance between developing individuals as individuals, and developing individuals [who will be] able to take on some of the most pernicious challenges that the world faces.

We have just 350 students, and about 17 percent come from the state of Maine. We have students coming from about 40 states and about 40 countries. But a third of them stay in Maine. So I really like the idea of COA providing a framework and a platform for helping the state of Maine as it grapples with its complex future.

IJ: There's not a lot of ambiguity when you're at the wheel of a ship—or is there?

Brennan: I do agree with the notion of ambiguity that they'll have to confront. And what concerns me is that, because of the collective mentality we see in the Millennial generation, because they get reinforcement in real time through Facebook and all the rest, there's kind of a herd mentality for arriving at answers.

And that presents some difficulties, in my estimation, for taking responsibility for actions. A lot of the stuff we do here has to translate to personal responsibility for actions. If you're on the wheel of a ship or you're commanding the

direction that the wheel [should] be turned . . . I point out at the orientation when we have parents here that the odds are that within weeks or months after their son or daughter graduates, they're going to be giving a life-or-death command to someone their grandfather's age. That's not the place to learn about personal responsibility and about leadership and about all of the elements associated with making decisions and being confident in the decisions you make.

I am concerned about how this generation arrives at collective decisions. That's not necessarily a bad thing. After Captain Hazelwood drove the EXXON VALDEZ ship up on the rocks, we have completely changed the way management occurs on a ship. Bridge management now is collaborative decision-making, so that's a good thing. We do find that many of these kids come here and they do work well in teams. That's really what the industry is doing.

But there still needs to be a sense of personal responsibility. And we start driving that home right at the beginning—your responsibility to your classmates, your shipmates, the town that you live within—it's extremely important.

I hope when they leave we've prepared them well to engage in society with that sense, that they're not just following the head in front of them, that they're making informed decisions, whether on the bridge of a ship or when they're going into the ballot booth.

Snyder: One of the things I see communities struggle with actively is how to engage 45 or 1,200 or maybe a few thousand in a collective decision. Getting up and managing a town is an incredibly brutal act of kindness in the sense that you never get thanked for it. And yet you have to have in you the sense that it's your turn, it's your time. It's your opportunity to step up and play the role that the community needs played.

What's interesting is that people who haven't had the opportunity of a place like MMA often don't get recognized by the current generation of leaders as somebody who should think about stepping up. A lot of times, the way this leadership transition stuff happens, is somebody says, "You know, Bill, I think you've got what it takes to run for this position. Why don't you think about running for the school board, or stepping up and being the head of the fishing co-op?"

Increasingly, people are afraid of stepping into those roles because of the ambiguity—because social media can

ERIC WAYNE

"You have to have the sense that it's your turn, it's your time."
—Rob Snyder

create the herd mentality that will squash a public vote, regardless of the rationale of it.

Collins: I didn't mean to suggest becoming comfortable in ambiguity means you can just kick back and let it swirl. Behind the wheel of a ship or running an institution, you have to make a decision. And frankly, I am quite envious of MMA in so many ways because I've had my own experience on boats. There are very complex decisions that need to be made very quickly.

Similarly, the way we've run our educational institution—the students, faculty, and administration management, the institution as a whole, which is a challenge in and of itself—[examples are] very few and far between where I, as president, can say, "This is the way it's going to be."

IJ: What result does that produce in a young person?

Collins: It's a tremendous boon. It is that confidence that Rob was talking about, like, "Hey, you should be the all-college meeting moderator. Step up and do that." That is based on the town meeting and how our governance system was originally set up.

Some might say we're worlds apart, between MMA and COA. We may get there in different ways, but there are actually a lot more similarities [than differences]. We do not produce sheep at either of our institutions.

Snyder: What advice would you give parents who live along the coast who are helping their kids think about the opportunities ahead of them? These kids can go make a ton of money fishing, and yet it's clear that when they have exposure to these educational opportunities, they would do far better not only fishing, but in life, for having had the experience of these educations.

Brennan: Back to the question of ambiguity. When I began with the fisheries service, I began in a research program on ships from the Soviet Union. I already had worked in the US Merchant Marine, and I knew how it worked, and I'm thinking, "Now how does it work on a ship in an egalitarian society? Do they take turns being the captain [laughter]?" I

got on board and found out that there's a captain and there's a wiper, and there's a lot of positions in between. It has to work that way.

That's what we're doing here. We're a lot more rigorous in a lot of ways, because we're trying to instill in people the sense that in the Merchant Marine world, there are people who have to have certain responsibilities, and they have to discharge those responsibilities or else everybody's life is at risk.

But you don't just learn that by showing up on the ship. You learn that through a program of leadership.

That helps these kids when they get back into these communities because they're not afraid of taking responsibility. At the beginning, they don't know what that means, but over time, that's what our program is. In fact, our students develop and administer our code of conduct. I'd like to say that they participate as fully equal partners in all the decision-making, but they don't; the board of trustees is still in charge.

But they do participate in making fundamental decisions throughout the institution. It's by design—probably for completely different reasons than at COA, but hopefully with the same outcome. We're preparing people to understand what it is to be a member of a society, whatever that society is.

Maybe it's being a member of the local fire department. This fire department, which I've been a member of since I was a kid, is hugely dependent upon our kids, as is the ambulance corps and all the rest.

I hope they're going to be good engineers, too, but I also hope they're going to be good members of society.

IJ: Let's move from the philosophical to coastal and island economies. Rob, the coast is doing a lot better than the rest of the state, but if the natural resource–based jobs decline in a big way, which we know is possible, if not likely, what are the knowledge, skills, and values that young people will need to make a transition?

Snyder: I don't have a crystal ball, but I certainly am excited about what I'm seeing in people creating businesses that align with a sense of civic duty or a sense of environmental responsibility, with a profit motive. I think some of the stuff we're seeing in terms of aquaculture, and shellfish and kelp, plays that role.

I think these things really do position us well as a coast. Obviously, the potential for wind energy offshore here is phenomenal, but it's going to be a while before that gets moving.

The people who are going to be successful, in my mind, they are as much the technicians—they understand the programming and building of this stuff—as they are the people

From left, Darron Collins, Rob Snyder, and Bill Brennan TOM GROENING

who can actually help communities to understand the costs and benefits of these opportunities, and help to facilitate the movement of these economic opportunities into our region.

We've been so fortunate to have such a robust fisheries economy for so long that in fact, we haven't had to think very hard about alternative ocean uses. I say this while recognizing that we've always been battling it out for ocean space.

But we're now in a period in which we're going to have to start reimagining what that ocean economy's going to produce. And that means thinking of it both in terms of the profit margin and the ethical commitments that we want to create, along with profit—whether it's a commitment to only doing things that add to the ocean, as we decide how to build out our harbors, as we decide whether or not to dredge, or whether we build energy infrastructure and where we put it. These discussions aren't going anywhere. We need the answer to the technology and the industry as much as we need the people who can move the discussion forward here. That's where the skill sets we're talking about, regarding leadership, really become incredibly important. Because the greatest invention on Earth is going to die on the vine unless we can figure out how to facilitate the social acceptance of it.

IJ: What's your best argument to a student, to a grad, for staying in Maine?

Brennan: I don't really have to argue. It's value, it's history, it's family connections, and frankly, it's been a change in the industry that recognizes that to have happy employees, you have to have happy families. By and large, the kids that leave here now, they're working in industries that bring them back home every couple of weeks.

Collins: I've got kids who came this year from Phnom Penh, Cambodia, and this is the first time they've seen snow, and it's such an incredible cultural change to be here. Yet, 30 percent stay, which is significant, not anything like MMA, and it's the opposite of what you see in a lot of the other institutions in Maine, the private ones, especially.

Snyder: We bring people in through our Island Fellows program and other consulting gigs, and what I think happens, for people who are not from here, is that if they can have one of their first formative work experiences here—to the extent that they have one of those major life experiences in this place, and the time here to have it, some sort of success—they'll just want to keep coming back to it. Even if they have to go away for 15 years to go into the workforce so they can afford to come back to it.

A lot of summer kids come back and stay; it's because they had some indelible experience here. And this place offers infinite amounts of indelible experiences. Because of the environmental beauty and the authenticity of people you can meet, and because it's somewhere special, it's not just anywhere. ♦

The Highliner's Choice

F or a fisher-
man—on the
water daily, subject to the
vagaries of weather—a boat is the
thin membrane between life and death.

Aesthetics in a fishing boat aren't the most important consideration. A rugged, well-built structure that's
"seakindly" and will get a fisherman out and back safely
and comfortably is. A boat's finish and appointments are
icing on the cake.

In the traditional plank-on-frame boats built by Peter
Kass and his small crew, fishermen get both top-notch
workmanship and elegant style. Some of the fleet's top
fishermen—"highliners," as they're called—have been
known to place an order with Kass immediately after
trying one of his boats. They don't mind paying up to
$500,000 for a Kass boat, and they have no problem
waiting in line, sometimes for nyears; none other will
do. And in the age of fiberglass, they're die-hard fans of

wooden
boats for
their ability to
deliver a comfortable ride.

The amazing thing is that Kass attracts
this devoted following—among both fishermen,
his largest customer base, and pleasure boaters—not
because he's doing anything particularly innovative.
It's because he practices age-old design and construction techniques with the highest degree of integrity,
turning out boats for customers he thinks deserve both
reliability and beauty.

Peter Kass boats are the Rolls-Royces of the lobster fleet

BY LAURIE SCHREIBER

PHOTOS BY MICHAEL O'NEIL

"I can't imagine anyone, no matter what trade they have, not wanting to do the best they can do," Kass says. "That baffles me. If you don't have your reputation and your pride, and everything to show for it, why would you even do it? I can't imagine saying, 'Oh, it's good enough.' Why would you? This product is you."

Kass doesn't seem to age. In his 50s, he's endowed with boyish good looks and a cheerful demeanor, possibly due to the fact that he loves what he does for a living.

Peter Kass at John's
Bay Boat Company
in South Bristol

"Sixty hours is a normal week," he says. "I spend about one hour a day managing my crew and two or three hours on the phone, buying materials. Then I work. About all I ever need to say to the guys is, 'Okay, you do this and you do that.'"

("I'm a cruddy husband," he adds. "I'm sitting there at the dinner table, and I'm thinking about the next detail at work.")

SHOWTIME

Last August, eight or nine Kass boats were rafted up at the Maine Boats, Homes & Harbors show in Rockland. Kass, the owners, and their families were hopping between decks for visits on a blazing hot Sunday. Among the fleet was Kass's latest, OUTER FALL, built for Spruce Head fisherman Jim Tripp. At 47 feet, it's the largest boat Kass has ever built. With a cedar-over-oak hull painted cherry red, bright-varnished sipo (an African wood that's an alternative to mahogany) interiors and furnishings, teak trim, paneled doors, and a Douglas fir platform (and fiberglass judiciously deployed along seams where freshwater can cause problems), it was also a gem-like standout against a backdrop of sparkling blue waters.

Tripp is more vagabond than businessman in his appearance. A bandana wraps his brow, keeping unkempt hair in place. He's not afraid of hard-used clothes.

"You're not going to get any truth out of me," he jokes, after greeting two other Kass boat owners, Steve Rosen and John Williams, aboard Rosen's boat, STAR FISHER. A lifelong fisherman, Tripp is a man who knows what he wants. Boats aren't just vehicles. You have to get to know your boat, he says—how it feels, how it maneuvers, what it will do in a big sea.

"You've got to pay attention," Tripp says. "Every little move you make, your boat does different things, different days. It's a learning experience."

Except for a brief stint with fiberglass, Tripp has always had wooden boats, including an Arno Day 36 and a Bobby Rich 43, named DAY STAR, which he bought secondhand to range offshore on overnight trips, hooking longlines.

In the 1990s, Tripp came across a Kass boat that struck his eye.

"I thought it had the prettiest lines I'd ever seen in a boat," he says. Two years later, he put in an order for a 42-footer. Named SEA WIFE, it worked out great for the next 20 years. "I loved that boat," he says. "I was never, ever scared in that boat. It's a good sea boat. It takes the weather."

A year ago, though, he decided it was time to get something a little faster and a little bigger for his trips offshore.

"You're making your big money when the weather can get really bad, November and December," he says. "You're fishing all winter in brutal weather, and you've got to haul when it's blowing 25, 30 miles an hour. You need something bigger."

Construction of OUTER FALL—named after an important fishing ground—began in July 2014. Tripp helped out the last couple of months of production, putting the rails on, sanding, caulking the deck.

"It's hard work," he says. "Everything's handmade. I felt bad when I took it. The guys who work on it, they put their heart and soul in this boat. You leave and they never see it again." Why is wood valued over fiberglass? The consensus is that wood provides a softer ride, absorbing vibration and noise, compared with the monocoque, drum-like nature of fiberglass that jolts a mariner's joints.

Or, as Tripp says, "It just feels human to me."

WOODEN BOAT MECCA

Kass got into boatbuilding for lack of a better idea, as he wryly says.

"Seemed fun. Got a job at a boatyard and really loved it."

Born in Massachusetts, he was always one to tinker and get his hands dirty as a kid. At 17, he "kind of ran away" to Virginia, where somebody who knew somebody got him a job that didn't last long. He found his way to Maine and started work at the Harvey Gamage Shipyard in South Bristol. It was the late 1970s, and Maine was something of a mecca, thanks in part to *WoodenBoat* magazine, for people who wanted to pursue wooden boat building in the face of the rise of fiberglass.

Gamage was building the 65-foot schooner APPLE-DORE. "There were three old-timers—real, lifelong, excellent boat carpenters," he recalls. "The youngest was 58, the other two were mid- to late 60s. Basically, us young guys would lug things for the older guys. And that was a super way to learn. We were right there with them. You couldn't get a better learning experience."

When Gamage switched to steel construction, Kass took a job at Goudy and Stevens in East Boothbay, where his duties ranged from large-scale repair jobs on draggers to working in the joiner shop. In 1982, he was hired at Padebco Custom Boats in Round Pond to help build a 30-foot Atkin cutter.

A year later, he stepped out on his own and opened John's Bay Boat Company in South Bristol, on several acres—with tidal frontage he says he never would be able to afford today. In the early years, his mainstay was repair work, while building small boats in the 20-foot range. He received his first big commission in 1986, a 42-foot

"I can't imagine anyone, no matter what trade they have, not wanting to do the best they can do."

Carroll Lowell design named SHARON ROSANNE, for a Portsmouth, New Hampshire, lobster fisherman.

"As soon as the boat was launched, people took notice: 'I remember the wooden boat I used to have, and that was a nice boat, and blah blah blah,'" he says. "Before you know it, customers were lining up. I didn't realize the demand was there."

Steve Rosen of Vinalhaven was an early customer. He's had a Peter Kass boat, named STAR FISHER, for nearly 20 years. At the time, Rosen says, Kass was the only show in town as far as building in wood.

"When I wanted another wooden boat, I turned to Pete," says Rosen. "He had a reputation for building great boats and for doing it on time."

John Williams agrees. When it comes to providing what is an essential tool for a business, integrity is critical.

"The bank asked me if I had a contract with him," Williams says. "I said, 'No. I shook his hand. That's all I need.'"

Williams, who lives in Stonington, commissioned a boat from Kass in 1995. In 2012, he traded up to a larger boat, featuring the gleaming mahogany cabinetry that's a Kass hallmark.

"As far as boatbuilders, there's no one better than Peter," Williams says. "His workmanship is immaculate."

Building mostly in the 30- to 40-foot range, Kass's design process starts when he carves a half model. For a more complex product like a yacht, he might hire someone to do computer drafts that make it easier for the customer to visualize the design and make changes. But most of his production is lobster boats, and design and construction remain fairly consistent, with one to two emerging from his shop per year.

"Lobster boats are pretty simple creatures, really," he says.

Kass's designs are characterized by a deeper V to the bottom and a sharper bow than many other lobster boats.

"To me, that makes a better sea boat," he says. "I think they go easily at slow speeds. If you want flat-out speed, and some guys do, you want something that will jump out of the water," he explains.

"You look at a lot of these modern designs, they're very flat-bottomed, and when they get going, the whole first 10, 15 feet of the boat is out of the water. And they go great! But I think on a choppy day, a fisherman will be much happier in one of my boats," Kass says. "As one of my customers says, 'This fast-boat stuff is cool, but lobsters were never caught at 20 miles per hour.' You've got to be able to stand at the pot hauler once you get there. You don't want something pounding at your feet."

Construction is all about one detail at a time, says Sam Jones of South Bristol, who recently retired as Kass's right-hand man after 25 years.

"Everything is thought out," Jones says. "We're not trying to reinvent the wheel, just sticking with what works in the design and the materials."

More than anything, Kass strives for the best—so much so that sometimes, looking at his costs, he realizes he's shot himself in the foot.

"Some of these details, after I'm done, I look at the timesheets, and say, 'Oh, my God. Well, we'll shave some hours off the bill,'" he says. "But I do always tell my guys, if I'm not around to make a call, assume it should be better, and if there's a money problem, I'll work it out. Either the customer is good with it or I eat some [of the cost] or whatever, but we don't want a quality problem. Never."

By now, Kass has built over 60 boats, about a dozen of them in Stonington, due to a cascading effect that happened when John Williams's father, Bob Williams, brought his first Kass boat to town 25 years ago. He currently has five orders lined up, which is five years' worth of work, unless he can find qualified employees to speed up the production schedule. That last point is difficult these days. Finding younger people interested in getting into the trade is his biggest problem.

"Impossible," he says. "Working in the trades doesn't appeal to young people anymore. I think it's because everything they know comes off that stupid glowing screen. I can't believe there aren't young people knocking on my door. Jeez, I can't wait to get to work every day."

What's lost, he says, is the sense of craft as a normal part of everyday life. Many people today refer to the "art" of wooden boat building. Sure, it's creative, he says. But it's just what people did—to work, to support a family, to live. Kass refuses to be called an artist. For him, the highest honor is to be recognized as an excellent and honest tradesman.

"These old codgers I used to work with, it was just there," he says. "They were craftsmen, but they didn't really think about it." ♦

Laurie Schreiber has written for publications in Maine and beyond for more than 25 years. Her new book, Boatbuilding on Mount Desert Island, *is a collection of historical profiles with a touch of contemporary activity.*

Ryan Larrabee's boat,
RESOLUTE, *at the 2015*
Stonington Lobster Boat Races
WALT BARROWS

Peter and some of his clients/
fans at the 2015 Maine Boats,
Homes & Harbors show

CORNERING THE ISLAND FUEL MARKET

Pete Pellerin took on fuel delivery
for Casco Bay islands,
and consumers won

BY JENNIFER VAN ALLEN // PHOTOS BY GABE SOUZA

Pete Pellerin at his home on Chebeague Island

When Pete Pellerin moved to Chebeague Island in 2009, he expected some basic necessities to cost more. But he wasn't prepared for the expense of propane to power his stove and heat his home. And even though he was juggling five jobs, he wasn't sure how he would afford it.

"I was blown away that someone could charge $175 to fill a 100-pound tank," he said. "And I couldn't imagine how everyone else on the island was taking it on the chin."

Pellerin's quest for a more-affordable alternative led to the launch of Maine Island Energy, which now delivers propane to approximately 2,200 residents on the Casco Bay islands of Chebeague, Peaks, Long, Cliff, Bustins, Great Diamond, and Little Diamond.

Pellerin is betting that by serving multiple islands, he can achieve the economies of scale necessary to offer lower prices and more-convenient service than residents have historically been able to get. Already, he has cut the cost of refilling a 100-pound tank from $175 to $135.

What's more, he has been able to leverage the logistics expertise he developed during a 10-year-career at UPS to get the fuel delivered faster, and reduce his own cost of doing business.

Pellerin stresses that he wants to fill islanders' unmet needs—he does not want to step on the toes of those who are already in the market.

"I want to honor what people have been doing well for years," he said. "And I want to work toward a good relationship that will help all islanders."

ISLAND MARKUP

Though propane prices in Maine were approaching five-year lows in late 2015, for islanders, fuel has long been more expensive, largely because of the cost and logistical hassle providers must shoulder, arranging barges and working around ferry schedules.

"Getting anything out there is going to be more of a challenge," said Jamie Py, president of the Maine Energy Marketers Association.

As a result, "Often, only one company ends up serving a community, and the lack of competition contributes to higher costs," said Suzanne MacDonald, community energy director for the Island Institute (publisher of *Island Journal*).

Given the relatively small and static size of island populations, suppliers have struggled to spread rising expenses over a limited base of revenues that have little prospect for growth.

"People have been doing it for years, one island at a time, and we all have the same problem," said Coley Mulkern, co-owner of Peaks Island–based Lionel Plante Associates. "[Larger providers] divide these costs up by a million customers. We divide it over 350. The volume never gets above a certain amount. And you can't just keep charging customers more."

The Island Institute has deployed a raft of initiatives to make energy more affordable (see sidebar below). But in the meantime, Pellerin's plan to aggregate demand has offered relief to many islanders.

"I'm thrilled to see what Pete is doing," said MacDonald. "He has the ability to build a market that's big enough to get economy of scale, yet still be community-oriented."

ISLAND HOSPITALITY

That observation bears out during a visit with Pellerin. He seems to embody lean efficiency, his moves crisp and precise. He doesn't walk. He darts. He speaks with intention and eye contact. It's as if the expertise he developed in efficient logistics during his UPS career has saturated his mannerisms, and seeped into his sinewy frame.

In an instant, he can tick off the exact number of footsteps required to refill a propane tank, and the number of minutes to allot for each delivery so he can be off the island before the tide recedes.

And yet he is as warm as he is deliberate.

Whether helping an elderly customer fix a pilot light, assuring another customer about a stove delivery, or orchestrating subcontractors, it's clear the calm confidence he brings to the work is as critical as the fuel he delivers.

Though relatively new to Chebeague, Pellerin exudes a fierce familial devotion to the island he adopted, and the community that has embraced him.

On a sunny day last September, as I tagged along on service calls, he proudly showed off the island sites where he has established roots—the point at Bennett's Cove where he and his wife exchanged their wedding vows, the home where his children were born, and the bulk propane dispensary he has established in the front yard of his current house, with capacity for 2,200 gallons of propane.

Since moving to Chebeague, Pellerin says, he's been overwhelmed by island hospitality, which reminds him of

Priming the Pump

The Island Institute has launched several initiatives to help reduce energy use and increase energy efficiency. In 2014, it helped to organize Community Energy Action Teams on seven islands to tackle energy issues and share solutions.

The Institute also coordinates "weatherization weeks." To date, 375 homes—15 percent of the year-round housing stock on islands—have been assessed for heat retention and given air-sealing fixes, which deliver an average savings of $300 per household per year.

In May 2015 on Matinicus and Monhegan, Island Fellow Ben Algeo led a campaign to outfit homes and businesses with LED lightbulbs, which use 75 percent less electricity than incandescent bulbs. The cost to residents was just $1 per bulb, thanks to rebates from Efficiency Maine, plus logistics, and a bulk discount the Institute was able to arrange with Newport-based Gilman Electric Supply.

Last November, 140 island residents, politicians, and energy-industry leaders gathered for the Island Institute's sixth annual Island Energy Conference in South Portland to exchange ideas, explore challenges and regulatory issues, and discuss the feasibility of alternative energy sources like solar power.

—JVA

the central Maine community where he grew up. "I felt accepted by the community immediately," he said.

While renovating his house with his wife, Becky, 17 neighbors showed up unannounced one day to lend a hand.

"I was just stunned," Pellerin said. "It was their way of saying, 'Welcome to the island. If we can help each other, we do.'"

And Pellerin, 47, has embraced the island. He expresses pride that his two children were born on Chebeague, and takes time to serve as a selectman and on the boards of the recreation center and Casco Bay Ferry Lines.

"I want people to be able to live on an island, and not have to struggle to survive," he said. "And I want my children to have the same opportunities I've had to live and thrive here."

LAUNCHING THE BUSINESS

Pellerin said his desire to make island living more affordable is largely what drove him to get into this business in 2009.

While working as a stern man, caretaker, and maintenance man, he became trained and licensed to install propane-powered appliances like water heaters and wall-heating units.

When Thibeault Energy shut down in 2011 and left some Chebeaguers without a propane supplier, he negotiated with Bath-based M. W. Sewall to deliver a propane truck on a barge. He bought the contents of the truck, then delivered it to 25 residents.

But it quickly became clear there might not be enough customers on Chebeague to sustain a business. And juggling deliveries with his other jobs was tough.

"You have to put a lot of oars in the water to stay afloat on an island," he said. "If I continued like that, I was going to break my arms."

Through ISLE, the Island Sustainability through Leadership and Entrepreneurship program, which the Island Institute offers along with the group Leadership for Local Change, Pellerin met residents from other islands who also were struggling to get, and afford, propane. He realized a multi-island operation would be more viable.

"There's been an imaginary border between the islands for generations," said Pellerin. "I had an opportunity, as a businessperson and community member, to tie the islands together."

Pellerin's expansion plan was welcome news for fuel suppliers who wanted to get out of the business.

Brad Brown had delivered fuel to 300 residents on Long Island since 1985. But in 2012, he became ill and was unable to continue. Brown's sister Towanda tried managing the business on a temporary basis, but she needed someone who could permanently manage the accounts, field service calls that came in at all times of the day, and handle the physical demands of the job, which often required hauling heavy tanks over rough terrain.

"I was pulling my hair out," she said. "It's a really tough business. And I could barely move those tanks."

She approached Pellerin, and was bowled over by the time he spent with customers to ensure a smooth transition. "He has been so good to so many people," she said. "He works very hard, and has never let a customer down."

Pellerin also acquired the oil and gas retail delivery operation from Lionel Plante Associates.

"It was time to start paring down the size of our company, and focus on excavation and barging," said Mulkern. "So when Pete said that oil and propane was the only business he wanted to be in, it was a great match. The more customers Pete can have, the more he can spread out all his costs."

To be sure, starting up has been a difficult and costly process. "There's a reason why not everyone is doing this," Pellerin said.

He has tapped his savings, loans from investors, and business revenues to finance necessities like insurance, equipment, trucks, and transportation, plus the cost of hiring five employees and five subcontractors, and installing three bulk propane tanks on his property.

But to many islanders, Pellerin has already been a great asset. Even beyond cost savings, his customers rave about the peace of mind he has provided by advising them on efficiency and safety issues, helping them to install larger tanks, and using online billing.

"Pete makes life easy on us, and the fact that he lives on the island is terrific," said Chebeague resident Jay Corson. "His prices are quite reasonable. And it's nice to see a youngish guy who is working very hard to provide this service." ♦

Jen Van Allen is a Yarmouth-based writer and author of four books, including Run to Lose *(Rodale, 2015). Her work has also appeared in the* Washington Post, Runner's World, *the* New York Times, *the* Portland Press Herald, *and* MaineBiz. *Learn more about her work at jenvanallen.com.*

ACADIA'S OFFSHORE ISLAND

Isle au Haut includes 18 miles of national park trails

BY ABIGAIL CURTIS // PHOTOS BY SCOTT SELL

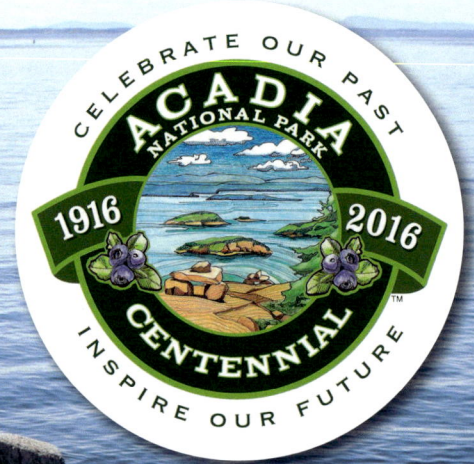

CELEBRATE OUR PAST
ACADIA
NATIONAL PARK
1916 2016
CENTENNIAL
INSPIRE OUR FUTURE

For generations, Kendra Chubbuck's family has called the dark spruce forests, cobble beaches, and rocky cliffs of Isle au Haut home.

Chubbuck, who moved to the offshore island full-time about four years ago, used to live in a little red house on the shore that was built in the 1930s by her great-aunt and great-uncle. The property was rich in beautiful views, although without modern conveniences like running water and electricity. One upgrade was a simple outdoor shower she installed on her porch.

But those beautiful views also were appreciated by the tourists who hike and camp every summer on Acadia National Park's relatively remote outpost on the

113-square-mile offshore island. They also parked their bikes in her driveway and hiked across her front yard, leading to the occasional surprise encounter.

"You have to look out the door to make sure no hikers are coming before you get out of the shower," Chubbuck said, laughing.

That's just how life goes on Isle au Haut, where fishermen and other islanders have to share their island—at least in the warmer months—with a few park rangers and about 7,000 park visitors every year. Acadia National Park is celebrating its centennial this year, as is the National Park Service. The portion of the park on Isle au Haut is often overshadowed by Acadia's presence on Mount Desert

Belfast

Castine

Blue Hill

Frenchman Bay

Winter Harbor

Bar Harbor

Egg Rk

Fl 10s 123ft 19
HORN

MT DESERT I

Islesboro I

Long I

Blue Hill Bay

Deer Isle

Jericho Bay

Swans I

mden

port

North Haven I

PENOBSCOT BAY

Vinalhaven I

Isle au Haut Bay

Isle au Haut

RO & G

Island, but not for its residents, who number around 40 in the winter and several hundred in the summer. Most have adjusted to having a national park in their backyard—but that hasn't always been the case since its creation more than 70 years ago.

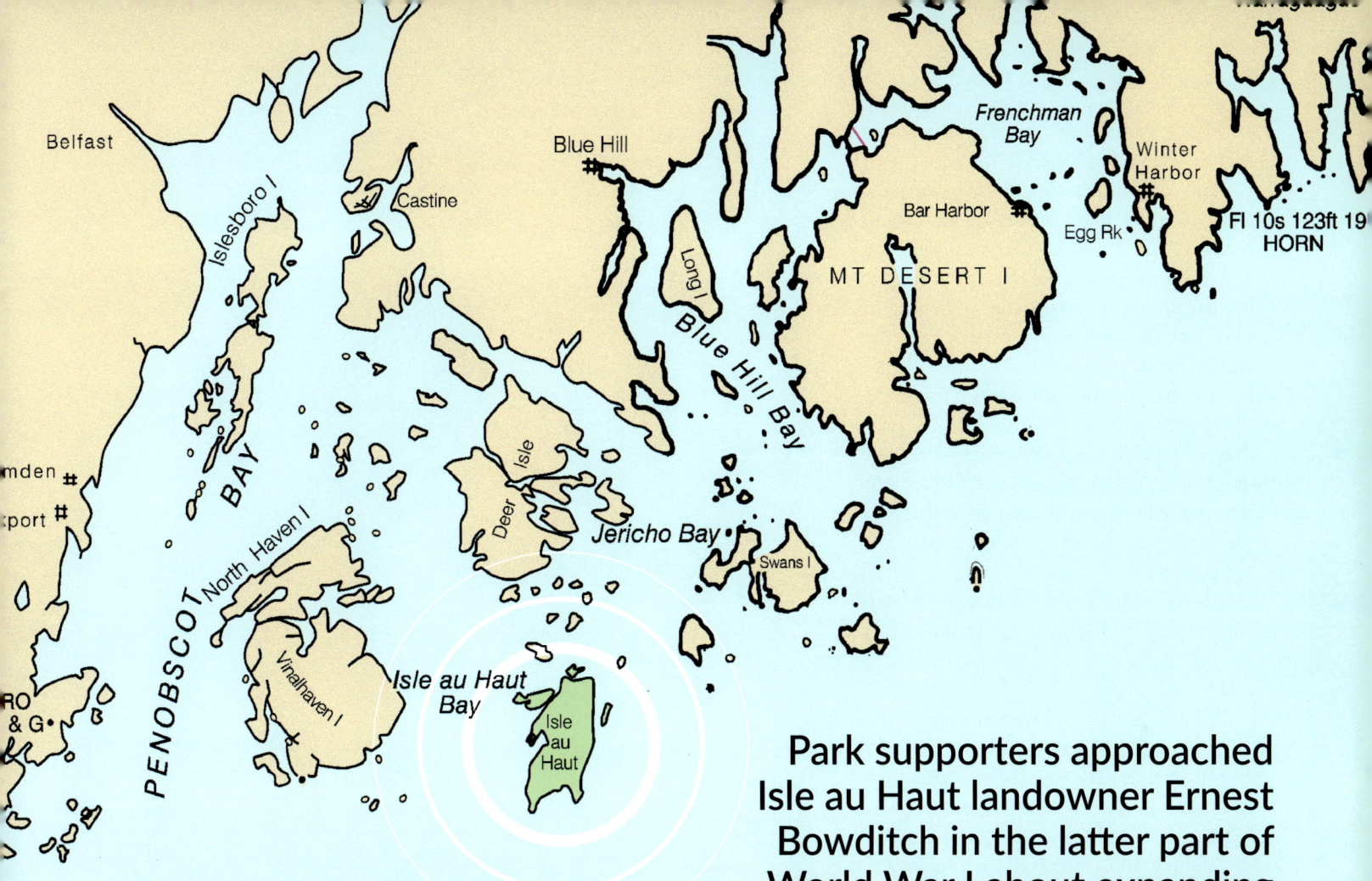

Park supporters approached Isle au Haut landowner Ernest Bowditch in the latter part of World War I about expanding to the offshore island.

ACADIA CENTENNIAL

Acadia National Park was first established as Sieur de Monts National Monument in July 1916. Three years later, its name was changed to Lafayette National Park, and it became the first national park east of the Mississippi.

Park supporters approached New England landscape architect and Isle au Haut landowner Ernest Bowditch in the last years of World War I about the possibility of expanding to the offshore island. At the time, Bowditch demurred. However, during World War II, his heirs did decide to donate a large tract of land on the southern part of the island to the National Park Service. The move came as an unwelcome surprise to islanders.

"It was a done deal before we knew anything about it," one islander recalled years later. "We were so mad."

Some of the year-round residents opposed the loss of the island's tax base and the erosion of local control, anthropologist Douglas Deur wrote in a 2013 community history.

Realities of island life are very different today than they were in the 1940s. The year-round population on Isle au Haut has been shrinking, and this year, only two children attended the one-room schoolhouse. Despite a generally sanguine relationship between the town and the park, some residents feel that sharing the island is not in the town's best interests.

Matthew Skolnikoff, a landscaper who has lived on the island year-round for 25 years, said the national park owns nearly half of Isle au Haut and pays $8,000 annually to the town in lieu of taxes. Another 25 percent of the island is owned by other tax-exempt entities.

"I'm not saying the park should pay full taxes," he said. "But when you have 75 percent of the island nontaxable, there's a lot of pressure on the rest of us."

Abigail Hiltz, a college student studying ocean and coastal resources in Galveston, Texas, also loves the island she grew up on and its national park. She is looking for a way to come back home for good, but on Isle au Haut, that's not necessarily easy.

"You're constantly thinking about the island," she said of life away from it.

And she knows the 18 miles of park trails like the back of her hand, having roamed over them in every season. She aspires to be an Isle au Haut park ranger, but her bone-deep knowledge of the island may not be enough to qualify her for employment.

"It's frustrating," she said. "You send them your résumé, your transcripts. Then they send you a questionnaire, and the first question is, 'Are you a veteran?' I think that living out here and having knowledge of the trails and the history of the island ought to be enough."

It's the same story for Patricia Barter, who moved to Isle au Haut at the age of 18 after falling in love with an islander and his home.

"I loved him and I loved this place," the 24-year-old said. "There's nothing like it."

Still, she needs a job. For two years in a row, she has applied to work for the park, but has run into the same obstacle as Hiltz.

"It's the most frustrating thing ever," Barter said.

PARK BENEFITS

Although the park has not turned out to be a big job creator, there are undeniable economic benefits. One is that park visitors help to keep Isle au Haut Boat Services afloat year-round. The Stonington-based company that runs the ferry is a lifeline to the island.

"A big portion of our income comes from transporting hikers to Acadia National Park," Captain Mike Moffatt said before piloting THE MINK back to the mainland. "It's a big help. The hikers, they subsidize this ferry service. It's a good thing."

Park ranger Alison Richardson shares Moffatt's assessment about park visitors. As an island resident who did manage to get into the park service, she has worked on Isle au Haut for nine summers, tending the trails and campsites and keeping an eye on the hikers. She is happy to share the island that she loves.

Isle au Haut park ranger Nick Freedman clears a trail.

Isle au Haut's mailboat, THE MINK, *full of summer visitors*

"I always just say, it's so different than Mount Desert Island. It's so much more remote and a little bit more wild, more primitive. It's definitely more quiet. I think the pristine, wild part is what I like best," she said.

The park's 18 miles of trails allow visitors to explore rocky shorelines, upland forests, bogs, and a mile-long freshwater lake. Park officials urge visitors to bring adequate footwear, warm clothing, and rain gear, to be prepared for rough and sometimes wet trails.

There are five designated campsites at the park's Duck Harbor Campground, available May 15 to October 15. Campers are limited to one stay per year. Visitors also can stay at the Keeper's House Inn, a restored lighthouse station built in 1907 that is on the National Register of Historic Places.

"It's really rugged and just gorgeous," Richardson said. "I think the people who have come out there have done their research. They're great people. They know what they're doing."

Every year, the seasonal rangers struggle to find housing on the island, and don't always succeed. One ranger last summer lived on the mainland and took the mailboat back and forth to work.

"That's why it would be so great to have a local group of people," Richardson said. "They live here. They know the island already," she said of Hiltz and Barter. "The past two seasons, one guy was from Utah. The other guy was from Joshua Tree [California], in the desert. They have to spend time learning the trails, the boat schedule, everything. Islanders would know everything already—and we could just get to work."

Some islanders think the presence of the park could do more for Isle au Haut's economic development. Before the 1980s, when the park service built a pier at Duck Harbor on the island's southern end, the only way to get to the park was by landing at the town dock and hiking for four miles. Islanders didn't always appreciate those visitors.

"There were a lot of people wandering through town, not really knowing where to go," Richardson said.

Now, with the new dock, most park visitors completely bypass the town. And Chubbuck, who owns Shore Shop Gifts near the town landing, wants that to change. She and others on the Isle au Haut comprehensive planning committee are trying to figure out a way to get visitors to spend an hour or so in town, so they can check out sights like the tiny post office and the church, and hopefully spend some money at the stores.

"We need some economic development in here," she said. "We've got to survive somehow."

Island living, and the unique challenges of Isle au Haut, are not for everyone. But for some year-rounders, the park is a big part of what makes their island special. Tucker Runge, a lobsterman, said that he uses the park all the time.

"I think I was the only one who hiked there last winter," he said. "It's nice to have it to yourself. It's just a really good resource to have." ◆

Abigail Curtis lives in Belfast and writes for the Bangor Daily News, *where she reports on such varied topics as Amish-made charcuterie, the renaissance of young farmers in Maine, and annual town meetings, Isle au Haut style. When not writing, she enjoys hiking, cooking, and working in the garden.*

Aquaculture's Next Wave

Mussels, oysters, and kelp emerging along Maine's southern coast

BY NANCY GRIFFIN

Casco Bay, dotted with hundreds of islands and stretching over 25 miles from Cape Elizabeth to Cape Small, is seeing an upswing in what could prove to be a new economic engine for the area—shellfish and seaweed farming.

"It's a really interesting area for aquaculture in the state," said Sarah Redmond, marine extension associate with Maine Sea Grant at the Center for Cooperative Aquaculture Research in Franklin.

"There's a wide diversity of companies growing different things, and it's next to the largest city in Maine. It's the busiest area in water-related business—shipping, recreational boating, fishing, ferries, tankers—and with year-round island communities," she said.

ALEXANDRA DALEY-CLARK

"Casco Bay, especially northern Casco Bay, has lots of diversity in temperature and salinity and a lot of variety in habitat, and these are the kind of locations people have been occupying in recent years," Redmond added.

Location is all-important for Maine marine farmers, said Redmond, because the largest expense can be transportation of products to market.

That's one of several reasons Peter Stocks, owner of Calendar Island Mussel Company, is growing mussels off Chebeague Island in Casco Bay. "We can harvest from a clean bay, drive product to Boston in a few hours, New York in twelve hours, and to Chicago in twenty-four hours."

Portland is an accommodating home port, he said, with the fish exchange, cold storage, and trucks to Boston every day—all key amenities. "We can buy tons of ice, and if we need a mechanic or vessel support services, it's there," he said. "That doesn't exist in other parts of the state," he added.

Because of the opportunity aquaculture provides for diversifying and stabilizing income for coastal residents, whether they've been involved in marine businesses or not, the Island Institute, publisher of *Island Journal*, has launched an aquaculture business development initiative. The project provides business support and marine resources technical assistance to 23 participants, 16 of whom are in the process of submitting lease applications

> # "We can harvest from a clean bay, drive product to Boston in a few hours, New York in 12 hours…"
>
> —Peter Stocks

to the Department of Marine Resources (DMR) or have already gotten approval to start farms. The goal is to support those working toward establishing kelp, mussel, or oyster aquaculture businesses within the next two years.

BUILDING BIGGER MUSSELS

Maine mussel growers are hoping to put a serious dent in the market share of Prince Edward Island growers, who currently dominate. "They produce thirty-five million to forty million pounds a year. We see their trucks crossing

Maine all the time," said Stocks, who also has a farm in Blue Hill.

But Maine mussels are prized for size.

"We command a twenty- to twenty-five-percent price premium over PEI mussels because of quality," said Stocks. "And because we're two to three days closer to the major markets, ours are fresher, and they're between fifty to one hundred percent bigger."

Calendar Island Mussels sells primarily out of state, though two Portland restaurants feature the product. Stocks plans to launch retail sales via the Internet.

Part of the appeal of being in the mussel aquaculture business is that once they begin growing, there is little for the owner to do. But rope-grown mussels constitute a pricier start-up business than, for example, oysters, explained Dana Morse, marine extension agent with Maine Sea Grant, based at the Darling Marine Center in Walpole.

"The equipment and capital involved are significant," said Morse. "You might sell fifty thousand oysters, compared to the hundreds of thousands of mussels you would need to sell [to cover costs]."

While mussels don't command as high a price as oysters, they do take up less space than oysters, and can be harvested nearly year-round.

"There's some seasonality," said Stocks. "We have to balance the needs of the farm-to-table movement with that of the natural cycles of the product, which is live, not frozen." Generally, he harvests from August to June. Red tide, a naturally occurring ocean algae bloom that comes in the warm months, often shuts down harvest in late June and for most of July.

The summer months are when maintenance is done on the water-based equipment, and when "seed" is collected.

"We don't purchase seed," Stocks explained. "We collect it on ropes," known in the business as "fuzzy ropes," in areas where mussel beds are close to shore. "Shellfish farms create a lot of larvae because they naturally exist in the ecosystem. One female mussel can produce one thousand to one million larvae."

Matt Moretti, 31, formed Wild Ocean Aquaculture to purchase Bangs Island Mussels with his father in 2010. He developed an interest in marine farming in graduate school for marine biology, "but I didn't think I'd do it," he said.

The Bangs Island Mussels crew moves mussels from the raft to the barge.
SCOTT SELL

A Basket Island oyster MARK GREEN

When he decided to try it, he began his career working on an oyster farm in the Damariscotta River.

"Finfish you have to feed; mussels are filter feeders, [meaning] they remove algae and other inorganic nutrients from the water," said Moretti, "so they improve water quality." He expects to harvest 200,000 mussels a year on his farm, which covers 3.6 acres (though only about 10 percent of the surface area is used). The state issues leases for aquaculture sites after holding public hearings.

The mussels are grown on ropes that hang 35 feet into the water from rafts, with around 400 lines per raft. Moretti does most of the work on a 40-foot barge, using net reels as lift lines. He lives on his boat—an old trawler—and brings the mussels back to a Portland wharf for processing. "I'm right here, all the time."

But Moretti's not sticking strictly to mussels. He's trying "integrated, multi-trophic aquaculture," defined as providing the by-products of one aquatic species as inputs—fertilizers, food—for another. In other words, "We're growing two species on the same site, and they benefit one another."

His second product is kelp, a kind of seaweed. "Both extract nutrients from the water. Both help improve water quality. We're able to produce a large amount of biomass with a small footprint," he explained.

OYSTERS ON THE FULL SHELL

Bob Earnest and David Whiston started Chebeague Island Oyster Company in 2013.

"Our original goal was centered on creating jobs, local and sustainable," Earnest recalled. "Our second goal is to make sure our activities, site selection and all, didn't interfere with lobstering." Both are board members of the Chebeague Island Community Association, and care about the town.

The first year, these "two old guys from away," as Earnest describes them, bought 50,000 spat (baby oysters). "The goal was to get the farm started, get young people interested," he said. The second year, they ordered another 50,000 spat, built up their supply of cages, built an upweller (a pump device that moves water upward to improve circulation), and acquired a couple of old boats.

"Year three, we ordered 250,000 spat," said Earnest. "We wanted to start out slow and learn. We intend to buy 500,000 next year, and level off there. In Maine, it's three to five years from spat to harvest." A young lobsterman has joined the business, and Earnest worries that it's hard on him because he works for "the other." Lobstering is the island's biggest employer, and "we made sure to stay out of their way."

"Maine is really well-positioned, arguably the best in the country."

—Mark Green

Last summer, they offered limited sales on the island to friends and family. When production increases, they still want to be sure the island is supplied first, before the other markets they hope to set up.

Mark Green, a Peaks Island resident, operates Peaks Island Shellfish and Basket Island Oyster Company. He's been raising oysters for three years and is nearing the harvest. "It's an absolute minimum of two years to sell an oyster. It's a long time to invest money and not get a return," he noted.

Green estimates the company has close to a million one-inch oysters, and in a year, after a good growing season, "We will have a lot of oysters."

He jokes that "You're not really an oyster farmer until you kill your first million oysters." When he has a steady supply, he plans to sell in Boston. Now he sells to Portland restaurants through a dealer. His oysters grow in suspended cages just off the seafloor, and while tiny, are also in bags.

"Maine is really well-positioned, arguably the best in the country," said Green, who has a PhD in oceanography and is still a professor at Saint Joseph's College in Standish.

"We can produce a lot, we have cold water, salt water, and the water is full of food."

His advice for those who want to farm shellfish: Have realistic expectations, and take longer than you anticipate.

Jon Rogers fishes for lobster out of Bailey's Island, but also operates Dogs Head Oysters, farming on the northern tip of Orrs Island, as of July 2015. "I signed up for a ten-week course at the Darling Marine Center. After the third class I went home and filled out an application for a four-hundred-square-foot lease," he said.

"I took a chance. Before I got the lease, I ordered seed from an outfit in Bremen. In early July, the seed was ready and I had approval for the leases," Rogers said. "If it works out, I'll be done lobstering."

KELP ON THE WAY

John Lewis has worked at DMR for 18 years, and in 2015 was made head of its new aquaculture division. When Paul Dobbins told Lewis in 2009 that he planned to farm seaweed, "I said publicly that he would fail," Lewis recalled. "Now I say publicly that I was one hundred percent wrong."

Dobbins started Ocean Approved Seaweed because he saw an opportunity in a burgeoning industry with high demand. He grows four kinds of seaweed: sugar kelp, horsetail, winged kelp, and "skinny sugar kelp," which "grows like a weed," Dobbins quipped. Growing seaweed is not the biggest challenge. It's a relatively low-tech, low-cost kind of aquaculture with a quick grow-out period. The bigger trick is creating quality products with market value.

"We develop products. Most aquaculturists grow and then market. First we developed products and created markets—then we grew."

The company received grants from the US Department of Commerce and the Maine Technology Institute to bring seaweed to a commercial scale. Dobbins chose to open-source all the resources employed in developing the farm—the methods and the technical information.

"It's all on our web page under 'sustainability,'" said Dobbins. "For anyone who wants to start farming, it reads like a cookbook." The company seeds long lines that sit seven feet below the surface, monitor weekly over the winter, and make sure there are no crossed lines.

The products are fresh-frozen, and now include a seaweed salad made with horsetail kelp; a kelp slaw; and kelp cubes, which are pureed frozen kelp, often used in smoothies. The markets are primarily school dining rooms, the retail dining facilities in hospitals, and restaurants from Portland to California.

Paul Dobbins of Ocean Approved holds up a strand of sugar kelp. SCOTT SELL

Dobbins points out that 95 percent of US seafood is imported, and more than half of it is farmed. The United States was slow to enter the industry: "We were the twenty-ninth country to farm seaweed, and the third in North America."

Worldwide, the seaweed industry was valued at around $6 billion in 2014, according to World Aquaculture, and most of the production goes to food products. Seaweed farming increased 50 percent around the world during the previous decade, even as wild harvest declined and demand outstripped supply.

Among the benefits of seaweed, said Lewis, are that "it's a winter crop, needs no fertilizer, doesn't conflict with navigation, sailing, or lobstering, or have an adverse visual impact."

The region is fertile for growing seaweed because of the nutrients, sunlight, "and the great current through our tides," Dobbins said. As for markets, "There's room for everybody, and more. We look at other seaweed companies as colleagues. The true competition is Asian imports. Ours comes from clear, cold water and theirs comes from the bays of Asian cities. Ours test free of heavy metals. I see no public studies on Asian seaweed, but a Korean news source said 74 percent of their harvest contained contaminants from Fukushima."

Moretti uses Ocean Approved's seaweed-growing method alongside his mussel farm.

"The two species on the same site have an effect on each other, and it's beneficial. We are still developing the kelp side of the business. We're selling directly to restaurants now, but we will ramp up and do a lot more this year."

The downside of seaweed farming? "Processing is problematic. Drying in volume is a difficult operation. Space and processing space are limited right now," said Lewis.

OPPOSITION

Strong opposition to shellfish and seaweed farms early on has largely diminished, observers say. While some lobster harvesters aren't thrilled about the farms, others, like Rogers of Bailey's Island, have gotten into it themselves.

Jeff Putnam, 37, runs his 45-foot vessel out of his home port on Chebeague. He's one of the island's 31 licensed lobstermen, and began lobstering right out of high school.

"I think the guys who have done the best job are those who reached out to the lobstermen prior to applying," he said of those getting into aquaculture. "That kind of pre-planning with local harvesters will work best. In the past, we've been hit with surprises. We'd just get an announcement of a formal public hearing."

Putnam is considering getting into aquaculture, and is taking part in the Island Institute's business initiative.

"The previous generation of fishermen could work in several fisheries. In my generation, that's not so possible," he said. "Being able to diversify will be important in order to make a living and continue to live on the coast of Maine."

The lease process takes at least two years, said Stocks. "That's a challenge for any aquaculture farm in Maine."

Lewis said DMR sends biologists to each site, maps the bottom, makes an underwater video, and then holds a public hearing. "We have ten decision criteria that must be met."

Sebastian Belle, head of the Maine Aquaculture Association, said his group began training commercial fishermen to raise cod, but admits it turned out to be the wrong species.

The training continues but now is more broadly focused. The coursework is 16 to 20 weeks long, one day a week, Belle said. "We start with the biology of the animals they will farm, get into science and environmental monitoring and marketing, business management, gear . . . It's comprehensive, but quick."

The goal is to integrate fishing and farming. "If new farmers are also fishermen, it contributes to healthy communities and healthy working waterfronts," said Morse of Maine Sea Grant.

Belle echoed that view.

"My beginning was commercial fishing, then aquaculture. It's completely and utterly natural for preserving working waterfronts," he said. "It's a good way to diversify the economic base of fishing families."

Some farmers are experimenting with other species, such as Arctic surf clams, razor clams, and sea scallops, said Morse. "I'm optimistic generally. It's a good thing; it can go a long way," he said. ♦

Nancy Griffin, a former journalist and native of Newfoundland, is a freelance writer living in Thomaston. Besides being a news and political reporter, she has covered fisheries, the seafood industry, and coastal issues for decades. She is the author of three books: Making Whoopies, The Remarkable Stanley Brothers *and* Maine 101. *Two more books will be published next year.*

We believe that energy storage shouldn't come at the expense of our environment.

The view from House Island across Casco Bay, toward the city of Portland, Maine. Courtesy Maine Solar Solutions

Clean energy systems need clean batteries.

Aquion saltwater batteries offer environmentally friendly solar storage without compromising on sustainability. Our patented Aqueous Hybrid Ion (AHI™) battery technology is a unique saltwater chemistry made from abundant, non-toxic materials. Our batteries contain no heavy metals or toxic chemicals and are non-flammable and non-explosive, making them the cleanest and safest batteries for your home or business.

Our batteries are the first and only in the world to be Cradle to Cradle Certified™, an esteemed quality mark for products made from sustainable materials and manufacturing processes.

Competing battery technologies have their drawbacks: lithium ion batteries can be dangerous, and lead acid batteries can be unreliable, maintenance heavy, and toxic. Aspen batteries are different because they're safe, sustainable, simple, and resilient.

Storing energy in Aquion Aspen batteries enables you to consume all the energy you produce and control your energy costs. That's why customers have chosen Aquion for nearly 200 fielded systems worldwide, ranging from a 4 kWh residential application to a 2 MWh installation that is helping an island in the South Pacific eliminate its reliance on fossil fuels.

When it came time to add storage to a renewable energy installation on House Island, the property owner worked with Maine Solar Solutions to find the best batteries for the system and the island. Finding a safe and maintenance-free storage solution was critical for the remote and sometimes inaccessible island location. Maine Solar Solutions selected and installed Aquion Aspen batteries, which, in addition to reducing the need for maintenance, allowed the property owner to reduce reliance on the diesel generator. With the lowest cost per kilowatt-hour over the lifetime of the battery system, environmentally friendly Aquion Aspen batteries were a perfect fit.

Left to right: House Island's 4.56 kW ground mount, powering the cottage and island wells; House Island's 13.4 kW array on the property's "energy building," where Aquion Aspen batteries are housed.
Courtesy Maine Solar Solutions

AQUION ENERGY

Choose the only safe and sustainable battery:
www.aquionenergy.com

David Vickery

The Poetry of Place

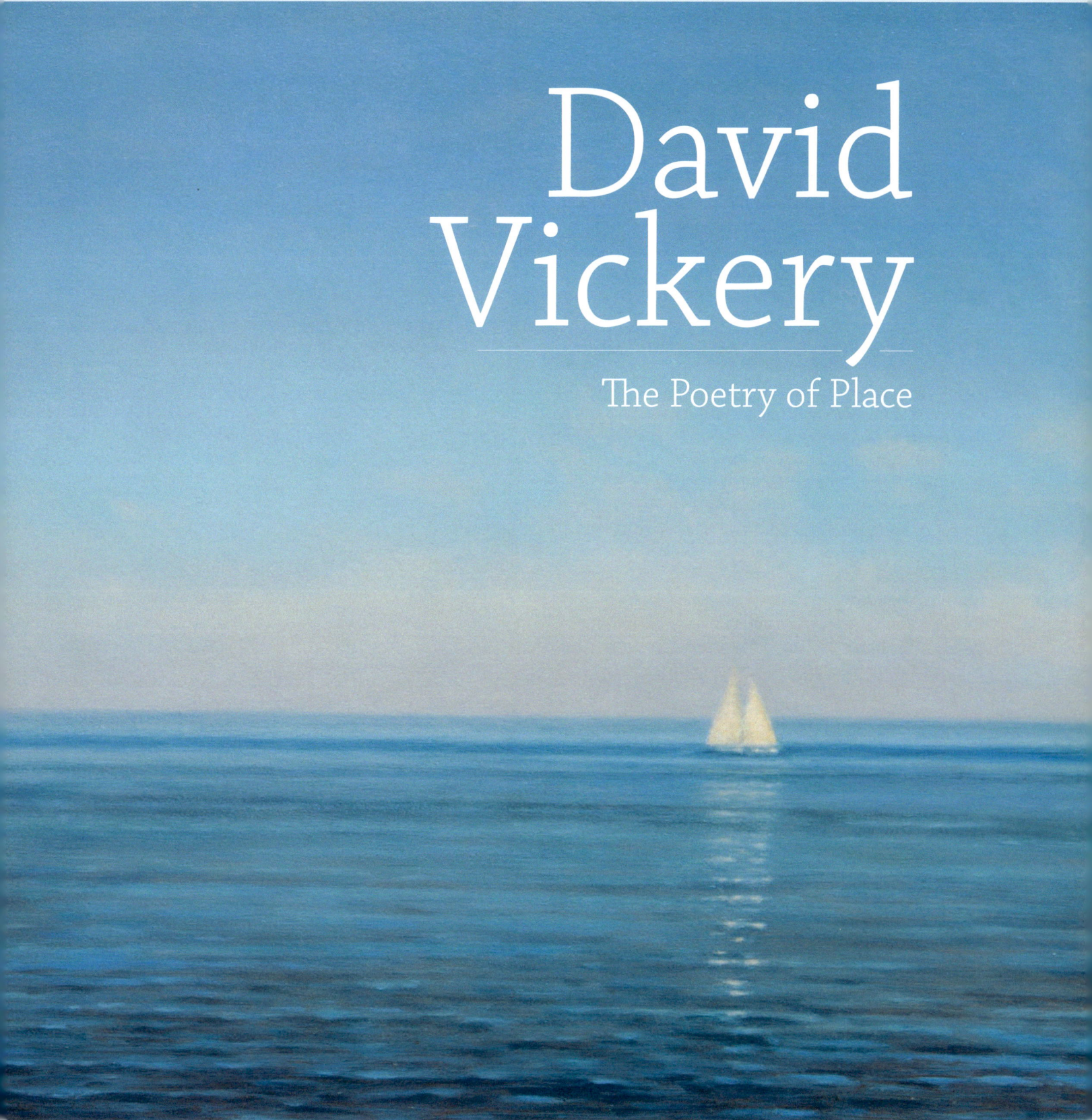

OFF BLACK HEAD (MONHEGAN) | *2015* | *OIL ON PANEL* | *12″ X 24″*

The painter David Vickery explores space: outdoor, indoor, around, above, across, beyond. He is equally expert at representing the parlor and the panorama, the intimate and the out there.

Vickery also loves light. There is a remarkable array on display here, from the glow of candles during a power outage to the luminosity of the night sky.

Vickery made his first trip to Monhegan in 1987 and in 1993 was awarded its Carina House artist residency. He has returned on numerous occasions, drawn to favorite motifs like Gull Rock, but also bent on exploring new subject matter. A pair of lawn mowers caught his attention during a 2011 stay. Turning away from the Rockwell Kent views of the island, the painter captured the handsome machines parked in a weedy lot on Monhegan.

With its curling piece of yellow paper, Vickery's "Message Board" recalls the trompe-l'oeil arrangements of such 19th-century painters as William Michael Harnett. Where Harnett and company focused on illusion, Vickery is more interested in the poetry of place, the why and where of this carefully realized piece of Maine.

The painter's home corner of Maine—the Cushing peninsula in the Midcoast where he has lived since 1991—seems to nourish realism. Alan Magee, Lois Dodd, and Nancy Wissemann-Widrig offer a rich variety of representational imagery, to which Vickery contributes his own special four-season vision.

In writing about his work, Vickery notes his tendency to integrate the natural world with the man-made. Going a step further in this self-assessment, the painter points to a need "to reconcile the inner, psychological world with the outer world of everyday experience and optical fact."

Such reconciliation is, paradoxically perhaps, often the source of the compelling intrigue found in Vickery's paintings: the empty wharf bathed in artificial light, the lobster boat anchored in the lee of a dark island. In melding the within and the without, the artist leads us to a fresh perspective on the world we look at every day.

—Carl Little

RECESSIONAL | *2011* | *OIL ON PANEL* | *23" X 11 ½"*

DESCENT | 2012 | OIL ON LINEN | 30" X 40"

MESSAGE BOARD | *2000–2012 | OIL ON PANEL | 11 ½" X 29"*

NIGHT WHARF (MONHEGAN) | *2011* | *OIL ON PANEL* | *16 ½" X 29 ½"*

CLAM DIGGER, MARCH | *2015* | *OIL ON PANEL* | *20" X 26"*

DAY-TRIPPERS, MONHEGAN | *2011* | *OIL ON CANVAS* | *30″ X 40″*

FALES', WINTER | *2009* | *OIL ON CANVAS* | *20″ X 36″*

MONHEGAN MOWERS | *2011* | *OIL ON PANEL* | *19 ½" X 15"*

JOHN'S WHARF II | *2012* | *OIL ON PANEL* | *18" X 18"*

David Vickery lives and paints in Cushing, Maine, and is represented by Dowling Walsh Gallery in Rockland.

Excerpts from The Poetry of Place *were written for the 2012 exhibition catalog for David Vickery's solo show at Courthouse Gallery Fine Art, Ellsworth, Maine.*

A Candid Conversation with Swan's Island's Candis Joyce

Island life imbues sense of community

BY TOM GROENING

Candis Joyce, 57, is director of the Swan's Island Educational Society (SIES), which is housed in a bright, attractive building constructed in 2011, and which functions as a combination library, museum, historical society, and learning center. In October 2015, when we talked, Joyce was winding down from the lobstering season, because in addition to heading up the SIES, she also works as a stern man two days a week on an islander's boat.

She's raised two children who were schooled on the island, and now has two grandchildren, the oldest attending the island school.

She grew up in Rockland as Candis Jellison, the daughter of a successful fisherman. Her father had ties to the island, and the family moved there when Joyce finished high school.

"We made the final trip from packing up the house in Rockland the day after I graduated from high school in 1976," she remembers.

IJ: How do you think living on an island has shaped you as a person?

Joyce: I think I've become much more community-centric. I find myself thinking about how things will help the community, rather than how they will help me or my family.

I think about when I first realized what a library really was—that it was a historical institution, that we actually preserve the island's history. And those two things together really formed a very powerful focus for me, because we not only provided information for the community, but we also collected historical information, stored it, and figured out ways to present it to people for them to enjoy.

That's probably one of the biggest benefits I personally have received. And I wouldn't have been able to say that years ago.

IJ: What's the biggest misunderstanding, or misconception, people have about island life?

Joyce: That the locals aren't very intelligent. Not the majority of people from away, but there is a significant group of people that appears to think islanders are not capable of helping themselves. And that's not true.

The other piece that I find very intriguing is that summer people come here when it's nice—when people usually go on vacation—and they wonder where we all are. Why we don't show up at committee meetings. Why we don't take part in events. Well, that's because that's when we go to work.

You know, you get up at four o'clock in the morning, and you need to go to sleep at eight o'clock at night, and you're just trying to maintain what you have to do. The seasonal residents on Swan's Island really would like to see us make some improvements—the town office, our government structure—and they want to know what, why, and how this all happens. And islanders just know how things work.

But summer people come to Swan's Island because they like it the way it is. We aren't commercialized, we aren't full of tourists. They like it quiet; they like that it's a fishing community.

And there's a good handful of the year-round community who can't see how fortunate we are with the seasonal residents that we have.

IJ: How do you get your groceries and other essentials?

Joyce: We have a food co-op out here. Some of us order Crown of Maine [a farm-to-table food service] through the store, and they get a standard markup for dividing up the case lots of squash, or whatever we decide to order, and then we go pick it up at the store.

Our new store owners, Brian and Kathy, are great, and they'll accommodate you with special orders.

I have an Amazon Prime account [which provides free shipping]; I use Amazon Pantry. And when I do go to the mainland, I go to Hannaford and the Belfast Co-op. I try to do as much [buying] on the island as I possibly can. I know Amazon isn't exactly "island," but it's $30 to go to the mainland. Plus gas. Plus at least one meal. And you have to add that to the cost of your groceries on the mainland. I'm not going to spend that much to go to the mainland to buy a bottle of ketchup.

IJ: So how many times do you go to the mainland in a year? How many ferry trips?

Joyce: Over the past couple of years, it's been more often. I used to go off if I had an appointment, then I'd do some grocery shopping. Or, my ex-husband and I, what we used to do sometimes was take the kids off and go to Subway and go to the movies on the weekend. But now, since I've reconnected with friends in Rockland, I tend to end up over there too much [laughs]. And I'm trying not to do that this year, because it costs a lot of money.

IJ: Do you ever think about moving off-island?

Joyce: [Nods]. To get a job. I think the thing that's causing the most anxiety in my life is not having a full-time income. And benefits would be great.

IJ: What do you think is this island's biggest problem—biggest threat? Gentrification, drugs, inability to make a living here . . . ?

Joyce: There are some of us who would like to continue living here who don't have the option of being a stern man, or don't have family that can help support them financially. They find themselves newly divorced, or there's illness in the family. There's not that second job that can help them support the household.

If you get a full-time job with benefits, you hang on to it, tooth and nail.

Drugs are definitely a problem out here.

You put kids in a boat, and they're making $20,000, $30,000 a year, more than their high school teachers. And they get an ache or a pain, or somebody says, here's this, and they get hooked on opiates, and they've got the money to pay for them. It's hideous, what it does to people.

IJ: Twenty years from now, what do you think will be the biggest changes that will be apparent here on the island?

Joyce: I'm hoping that you wouldn't see a lot of difference. That it would still be a working harbor, that people would still be able to have whatever they want in their own front yard. We wouldn't have any zoning except those things that really help us protect the land and water.

I would like to see a wider economic base and a little bit more visionary leadership in the town, to look at ways to encourage people to move here. And part of that's going to be much, much better Internet service and lower utility rates.

But I guess the only thing I would like to see is more of the houses lit up, year-round. And to do that, we're really going to have to come together as a community and have some hard conversations about what it means to be Swan's Island, and how we keep that same social, cultural structure in the 21st century.

IJ: Last question: What's the most annoying question islanders get asked by summer folks and visitors?

Joyce: They'll ask, "Do you have running water and electricity?" ♦

Vinalhaven's Investment

Town hired manager with scant experience, and has no regrets

STORY BY TOM GROENING
PHOTOS BY SCOTT SELL

For an island community that's a 75-minute ferry ride away from the mainland, Vinalhaven has been fortunate to have had two very successful long-term town managers, says Emily Lane, a current member of the island town's board of selectmen.

Sue Lessard served from 1993 to 2000, and then Marjorie Stratton held the job from 2002 to 2014.

Both remain well-regarded in the community, even though each had different strengths.

But in mid-2015, the town found itself without a manager. Steve Eldridge, hired in December 2014, left the job abruptly for a position in southern Maine.

What the town did next might seem rash, or ill-conceived, or even risky. But in hiring a 28-year-old without the typical public administration degree or much municipal experience, Vinalhaven showed a kind of leadership, betting not only that the young man would grow into the job, but that the qualities he brought to the town office might just trump what a veteran municipal manager could list on a résumé.

"I think we were quite forward-thinking," says Lane. "Not only the selectmen, but the community."

To understand why Vinalhaven hired Andy Dorr, you have to understand the process that led to Dorr not getting the job the first time around.

Stratton left the post in 2014, but had given the town ample time to plan for her successor. Using the Maine Municipal Association (MMA) as a consultant, the town created a 10-member committee to articulate what it was looking for in the new town manager. A staffer from MMA wrote a job description based on the committee's work, and the position was advertised.

"We had a basic idea of what we wanted," Lane remembers.

More than 100 applied. The MMA staffer winnowed that number down to 20, and the island committee further cut the list to 10 finalists. All were invited to the island for interviews.

"We were looking for that perfect person who would reach out to the community," she said, "but who also had a strong financial background."

While that process unfolded, Dorr was asked to serve as interim town manager. He had impressed selectmen and others with his handling of the town's comprehensive plan, shepherding it to public approval. That work was his focus as an Island Fellow, the internship program run by the Island Institute (publisher of *Island Journal*).

"You just say 'yes' to every invite. I couldn't afford to say no."

—Andy Dorr

For selectmen and members of the community at large who served on the screening committee, Dorr was a strong second choice.

"Andy had all the attributes that we wanted," Lane recalls, including a knowledge of and passion for Vinalhaven's unique charms, assets, and challenges. "But he lacked that financial background."

After Eldridge left, the thought of starting an exhaustive search all over again was daunting. So selectmen made what might seem like an old-school, from-the-gut move: They hired the young man who had been one of the runners-up for the job.

SMALL-TOWN GUY

Dorr hails from Waterville, a small town in upstate New York. He'd earned a two-year degree at a community college, studying criminal justice. After a year off, he enrolled in the State University of New York's College of Environmental Science and Forestry in Syracuse, where he earned a BS in environmental studies, with a concentration in policy, planning, and law.

Andy Dorr talks with Lisa Shields in Carver's Harbor Market on Vinalhaven.

Andy Dorr works with Emily Cohn's sixth-grade class on a sea-level-rise project.

Dorr arrived on Vinalhaven in the fall of 2011 for the fellowship. Being single and in his twenties, Dorr recalls watching the ferry leaving with his parents aboard. Laughing about it now, he remembers the finality of being island-bound sinking in, and asking himself, "What have I done?"

But he began exploring Vinalhaven's hiking trails, and joined a men's book club—and just about every other social group.

"You just say 'yes' to every invite," he said. "I couldn't afford to say no."

The work at hand—updating the town's comprehensive plan—would take a lot of time and effort. The state requires plans to be current, and often, towns are not eligible for state grants if the plan is out-of-date.

A previous multiyear effort to update the document, which identifies assets, resources, challenges, and goals, ended with islanders voting it down at town meeting.

Dorr's approach to the project is telling about his people and political savvy. Though the plan is not zoning, it can be the blueprint for new land-use regulations, and that can make locals nervous.

Dorr kept people informed, a strategy he described as "not putting people on their heels," a way to present information without making people defensive. And he listened.

"I tried to make an effort to identify who was against it last time, and get them to talk about it," he said. Some of the gripes about the previous plan involved small matters,

Dorr said. "Well, it's easy to not include some of those [provisions]."

Previously, the update was seen as driven by summer residents. To reverse that perception, "we did a lot of working groups in the winter," he said.

"My job was to understand the island. I'd talk to anyone who wanted to talk," he said.

But being town manager means more than understanding the people and their values. Vinalhaven's annual municipal budget is about $1.8 million; the school budget is about $3 million, and the town pays about $500,000 each year to the county. It's a serious business, requiring real financial skills.

IMPRESSING THE LOCALS

Lane, who has served a half-dozen terms as selectman in the 45 years she's lived on the island, said Dorr came close to being hired after his stint as interim manager.

"Barring his lack of financial experience, he would have been our choice," she said.

And Dorr understood the town's trepidation.

"I was grateful to have the six months [as interim manager]," he said. "I couldn't find any fault in not getting it."

Phil Crossman, now a selectman who was on the screening committee the first time Dorr applied for the manager job, is a supporter.

"He really had, by the time he applied for the permanent position, settled nicely into the fabric of this community and acquired a good understanding of much of what makes us tick," he said. "His having done that so capably gave us the courage to take a chance on his growing in the job."

Kris Davidson, an island real estate broker, was one of Dorr's advisors during his fellowship.

"We could tell he had all the qualities to fit in and be a leader," she recalled, when island leaders interviewed him for the fellowship. "He's very approachable, very likable, which is really important when you come into a small community." She also saw "a lot of confidence," tempered with a genuine humility.

Kathy Warren, the school business manager who worked at getting a Fellow on the island to tackle the comprehensive plan, gives him high marks, also noting his approachability. Throughout the comprehensive-plan work, Warren said, "He was very good about putting the responsibility for choices back on the townspeople."

Dorr was not shy about approaching people to solicit their views, and then took to heart what they said. "He's done a good job of really advocating for what he's been told by people. He's just a nice guy," she concludes.

Dorr loves the job.

"You never know who's going to call or show up in the office. You wear so many hats—treasurer, tax collector, general welfare administrator."

Along with day-to-day tasks are big projects. "We're looking at a new public works garage right now," he said. Being the team leader on such work "is the best part," he says.

"There's a lot of pride in the community," he continues. "It's nice to walk into a shop and have the shopkeeper know your name. It's a very independent, hardworking community. I think it's really a treasure."

Now that he's on board full-time, the town is investing in Dorr's education. He's enrolled in the University of Southern Maine's policy, planning, and management program at the Muskie School in Portland, attending classes there and online.

The decision to pay for the classes, which will give Dorr a master's degree, was unanimous among selectmen, Lane said.

The town sees its investment in Dorr's continuing education as an investment in the island's future.

"We hope he stays," Lane says. ♦

Emily Lane is a member of the Island Institute's board of trustees.

Tom Groening is editor of Island Journal.

ONE DEER, TWO ISLANDS

Hunting on Frenchboro creates logistical obstacles unlike any on mainland

STORY AND PHOTOS BY SCOTT SELL

Zach Lunt's hands are covered in blood and bile and fur.

"The fun part is over for me," he says, midway through field-dressing the buck he just shot. "It's all work from here on out."

But the work will take far longer than he thinks: Even though the kill was quick and easy, trying to make it legal won't be.

• • •

Earlier on this November morning: After bacon and eggs and coffee, Zach and I walk silently through the woods of Frenchboro, only stopping to inspect a deer trail or hoofprints or scat. The plan is to walk east from the gravel pit in the middle of the island to the back side of Rich's Head, where the wind won't be blowing quite so fiercely. Sunlight has just started to filter through the pines.

I have a bag packed with snacks and water and layers of clothes and lots of camera batteries, prepared for sitting in a blind for hours, waiting.

But we don't even make it to the Head. Just after coming down to the isthmus of beach stones that connects the Head to the rest of the island, Zach pauses for a second, shields his eyes from the sun's glare with his hand, then takes up his shotgun, gives the scope a brief glance, and fires between two trees. I hadn't even seen the deer.

We walk over to where the deer lies. A three-point buck, his fourth antler broken. Zach hit him in the heart and he dropped where he stood. He's still taking his last few breaths.

"Let's leave him be for a minute," Zach says.

• • •

At the crest of the hill overlooking Rich's Head, Zach takes in the field below, old cellar holes from a settlement that was once here, now covered with puckerbrush and skunk spruce.

"This won't be quite as long of a day as we thought it would be," he says.

He's a little disappointed. He hasn't seen a single deer all season and now, in the first 20 minutes of hunting, he's reached his limit for the year.

Zach, along with his brother Nate, grew up on Frenchboro. They know every inch of the island, roughly two-thirds of which is preserve land. Their father started taking them hunting when they were young to scout out good spots, and to teach them how to shoot.

"I might have been a little loud and impatient," Zach says of those first forays into the woods. "Patience is a big part of it. I think I've gotten better at that as I've gotten older. You realize that the waiting around is the best part."

Like many hunters, Zach feels the sport is less about killing an animal and more about being outside and feeling the rhythms of nature, as well as having a day off from lobster fishing and away from the stresses of raising five kids and tackling a list of house repairs. But on Frenchboro—eight miles from the mainland, with just three state ferry trips a week—it's also about subsistence.

"I don't think you have to go back too many generations to get to where they depended on deer meat," Zach says. "It's still a big part of our diet, to make ends meet. We don't have a store, and there's not a soup kitchen here in the wintertime. It's a meat you can harvest right here."

• • •

Zach folds up his knife and washes his bloody hands in the water lapping up on the beach of Eastern Cove. Then he texts his wife, Laurette, asking her to wake up their 15-year-old son, Austin, and send him clear across the island on the four-wheeler, to help haul the deer back.

When I first met Austin, the couple's youngest son, he was an impish second grader at the one-room schoolhouse where I, as an Island Institute Fellow, helped teach him and a dozen of his classmates. Now here he is, almost as tall as I am, but the same island kid.

"I thought Mom was kidding," he says, working with Zach to tie the deer on the back of the four-wheeler.

Austin had his first day of legal hunting on Youth Day this year, a few days before the regular firearms season started. With Zach's assistance, he had a head shot lined up on a buck near the apple trees around the harbor, fired, and the deer ran off. They tried to track him, with no

luck. But a quarter-mile away, they found three small drops of blood on a leaf. They figured the shot must have grazed him somewhere.

"Look, Austin!" Zach says, feeling around the top of the deer's head. "There's a scar! Must be the one you nicked a few weeks ago."

Austin smirks.

"Glad I didn't get this one," he says. "Means I wouldn't have gotten that big buck."

Earlier in the season, Austin got a sizable eight-pointer along the Gully Road, and doesn't miss the chance to remind Zach of his success.

"Okay," Zach says, starting up the four-wheeler. "See you back home." Zach drives halfway up the hill, but there isn't enough rope to secure the deer and it starts to slip off the back of the four-wheeler. Without saying anything, they start scouring the beach for additional rope. Luckily, the beaches here are covered with lobster gear and buoys, with plenty of rope for the taking. They secure the buck and Zach disappears into the trees, his blaze-orange vest and hat glowing in the dark of the woods.

• • •

In front of Zach's house, several fishermen stop their trucks and get out to take a look at the deer. Many are hunters themselves, and they trade thoughts about the patterns of the herds and the spots on the island where they've seen traces of activity.

For years, most of Maine's islands did not have deer-hunting seasons, and finally, the numbers got out of hand, with upward of several hundred on one island. On Frenchboro, many became incredibly tame. Zach remembers deer eating bread out of people's hands.

And they weren't healthy. Interbreeding produced albino deer. There wasn't enough greenery to keep them fed, and nobody could grow anything in their gardens, because the deer ate everything in sight, using garden plots as their toilets. And then there's the increase in Lyme-related illnesses

in recent years; in Zach's family alone, his wife, twin sons, and sister-in-law all have Lyme disease.

When hunting was finally legalized on the island in 2000 as part of a wildlife-management plan that several island communities adopted, hunters were allowed to get up to six deer for the first two years. Buck or doe, it didn't matter. The idea was simply to thin the herd, and they succeeded for the most part. But as the number of year-round Frenchboro residents decrease and guys like Zach struggle to find time to hunt, the deer population has swelled once again. You drive around at night and the headlights of your truck will pick up half a dozen standing in the middle of the road, eating fallen apples.

• • •

Zach takes the deer down the boat ramp to rinse it off in the shallow water of the harbor. Then, with Austin's help, he strings it up in his fish house.

The sun that was warm and welcoming earlier this morning has all but disappeared and the wind is picking up again. Time for another cup of coffee.

Around the kitchen table, I ask about tagging. Every county in Maine has a handful of tagging stations where hunters are required to fill out paperwork and pay a $5 registration fee, to make the deer legitimate in the eyes of the state. Of course, on the islands, it's easy to get away with bypassing this altogether. With no game wardens—let alone a police force—on Frenchboro, who would ever know? But Zach wants to do the right thing. As his kids start to hunt on their own, he wants to set a good example.

"I know for a long time the tagging was done at John's house," I say.

"Yeah, now it's at my brother-in-law Mikey's house. He's in Machias and won't be back until tomorrow. Gotta have it tagged within eighteen hours of shooting it, but that'll be close enough."

"You know," Laurette calls out from the next room, "I don't think Mikey will be back until next week, after Thanksgiving."

"Oh, boy," Zach groans.

Taking it to the mainland would mean an hour-long trip to Bass Harbor on Zach's boat, loading it into the bed of a borrowed truck, and another half-hour to Trenton. And then in reverse, the deer in tow. Out of the question.

Zach is immediately on his phone. After texting a few guys on Frenchboro, he calls Les at Underwater Taxi, a wharf and store on Swan's Island.

"Hey, you know who tags deer over there?"

The fishermen's co-op does, and 20 minutes later, we're on the ANGELA ROSE, Jay Fiandaca's lobster boat, which he's taking over to Swan's to show to a potential buyer. The deer

fits easily on the stern end, Jay's dogs taking turns sniffing at it.

When we pull up at the co-op, there are cheers from the wharf, people congratulating Zach. He steps off the boat and pulls out his wallet, faces us, and grimaces.

"Left my hunting license on the kitchen counter," he whispers.

"Geez, Zach!" Jay says, laughing. "This just isn't your day!"

"Maybe I can sweet-talk 'em," Zach says, walking up the ramp.

Inside the co-op office, Kenny begins putting the paperwork together while Zach describes the hunt, the size of the deer, his reason for being over here to tag.

"But you'll never guess what I did," Zach says slowly.

"What?"

"Forgot my license at home."

Kenny shakes his head and drops the forms.

"Can't do it then. Can't tag it without that little piece of paper."

Maybe Paul Joy, who's about to leave for Frenchboro to show the new mail carrier the route, can pick it up from Laurette on the town float?

"He won't be back for more than an hour, and we're supposed to close in twenty minutes."

"Can she send a photo of it on the phone?"

"Nope."

"Got a fax machine?"

"Yeah, upstairs."

"And that's legal?"

"That'll work."

A couple minutes later, the fax comes through with a copy of Zach's license. They get the paperwork in order and walk outside to put the tag—nearly identical to the state-issued plastic strips that are looped through the wire mesh of their lobster traps—on the deer's hind leg. But the boat's gone. Along with the deer. Jay had figured the paperwork would take a while, one of the co-op workers tells us, and has headed into the middle of Jericho Bay to show off the boat.

"Well," Kenny says, "guess we'll be here a while."

Although it's lunchtime and he's off the clock for the rest of the day, Kenny is legally bound to tag the deer now that it's registered on paper.

So we wait.

Not in a tree stand or a ground blind or even in the woods, but on a wharf, waiting for the red of the ANGELA ROSE to appear around Hockamock Head, watching as Swan's Island lobstermen stack traps in the back of their trucks. ♦

Scott Sell is the Island Institute's media specialist and a former Frenchboro Island Fellow.

Zach and Kenny finally tag the deer.

Babies on Board:
Islands Celebrate Family Growth

STORY BY COURTNEY NALIBOFF
PHOTOS BY WILLIAM TREVASKIS

Little Urchins daycare on North Haven

Playing outside of Island Village Childcare on Vinalhaven

I recently attended a three-year-old boy's birthday party on North Haven, where I live. His family's sloping lawn was overgrown with kids. One-year-olds rolled on the grass while toddlers bounced on trampolines. Slightly more sure-footed preschoolers bombed downhill on tiny bikes or climbed the tepee poles.

For those concerned about island communities, a scene like this is so much more than cute and heartwarming; it encourages us about our future. When couples have and raise children on islands, they are ensuring that there is a future.

There is more evidence than the birthday party that islands are fertile ground for the next generation. Both classes at North Haven's Laugh & Learn Preschool are brimming with children. In fact, the one- to three-year-old class was started in March 2015 to accommodate what appears to be a Fox Islands baby boom.

"It does seem to me that more than any other time since I've lived here, young people are choosing island life deliberately," says Christie Hallowell, Laugh & Learn Preschool's director. "They like the qualities and aspects, the comings and goings of island life, especially as the world changes. They want to bring up their children in a place like this."

Vinalhaven's Island Village Childcare had 22 students enrolled in late 2015, ranging from six-week-olds to five-year-olds.

"It was a long winter. It happens every so often," says Megan Day, director of the Vinalhaven child-care program. "It's like a cycle."

Calling it a baby boom might be hyperbole, but North Haven and Vinalhaven aren't the only islands seeing babies and toddlers as new year-round residents.

Just north in Penobscot Bay on Islesboro, 18 babies were born in the period from 2011 to 2015, with two born on the island.

On Cliff Island in Casco Bay, there are four children, ranging from ages five to nine, in the one-room school, and on Long Island, three babies were born in the second half of 2015.

On the Cranberry Isles, which includes Great Cranberry and Islesford, two babies were born to islanders in 2015, three in 2013, and one in 2010. Swan's Island, town

Foy and Lydia Brown with their children Cyrus and Rita

are thrilled when families with children choose to make an island their home.

GIVING BIRTH ON-ISLAND

There are no hospitals on Maine's islands, but that doesn't stop some from choosing to give birth at home. Sarah Poole, 34, gave birth to each of her three children in her own home on Vinalhaven.

"I was born here, and it was just something I always wanted to do," she said. "The doctor here at the [Vinalhaven] medical center used to deliver babies," she said. "I think for insurance reasons they stopped, and then people got in the habit [of going to the mainland] and thinking that you have to go to the hospital to have a baby."

Poole worked with Morningstar Midwifery, a Belfast-based practice with two certified professional midwives. The midwives visited the house prior to Poole's labor beginning, and left a birth kit at the house. They returned when she went into labor.

"They make arrangements and come to the house and hang out if they have to. With my first one, they hung out for two days because it was a long process," she said.

As with much of island life, sometimes the best-laid plans go awry, Lydia Brown remembers.

When Brown's daughter Rita was born, "the midwives didn't quite make it in time," she remembers. But in a way, that's a family tradition. Both Brown and her sister Thena were born at home on Vinalhaven and attended high school on North Haven. Both returned to the islands to farm and write after college.

When Brown had her first child, Cyrus, who is now seven, at home on North Haven, Morningstar's midwives were able to attend.

Rita, born without the assistance of midwives, was small but healthy. Although the circumstances could have been frightening, Brown accepted it as part of the deal. "I felt like it was the risk you take living on an island. You could have a stroke or a heart attack, and it was a factor of island living I accepted," she said.

clerk Gwen May joked, had a baby boom, with five born in 2011, three in 2012, four in 2013, three in 2014, and two in 2015. And on nearby Frenchboro (also known as Long Island), two babies have been born in recent years.

On Isle au Haut, just one child was born in the last few years, and it was to a family that had been seasonally on the island but may be moving out permanently this summer.

When island populations include children, schools stay open. When schools stay open, it's easier to entice other young families to move to an island. Island leaders

"It's a sense of pride thing, being born here," Brown said. However, not being born on-island isn't an impediment to being accepted. This, happily, seems very true. My husband and I moved to North Haven in 2005, when Waterman's Community Center was first opening its doors to preschool children. There was no day care available, but we hadn't yet considered having kids.

We got married in 2012, and I became pregnant in 2013. My obstetrician sister and obstetrician father were insistent that I plan to have my daughter in a hospital.

Since I was determined not to be in labor on a boat, I went to the mainland a week before my due date. I assumed the baby would be fashionably late, but I went into labor two days early, prompting my husband, who was still on-island, to frantically run onto the ferry with our dog and his overnight bag, but without our car, which didn't make it on, or my carefully packed hospital bag.

I labored at my best friend and doula's parents' house in Owls Head until I thought the baby might fall out onto their nice, clean floor, and we jumped into her car and took the longest twenty-minute car ride of my life. Once we arrived at Pen Bay's Women's Health center in Rockport, and it was determined that I was in transitional labor, we dashed across campus to the hospital, and within two hours, Penrose Claire Trevaskis was born. Her arrival was extremely normal, but I hemorrhaged after delivering the placenta and was grateful to be in a hospital and not facing emergency transport in a boat, plane, or helicopter.

Penrose plays every day with the five other kids in North Haven's class of 2032. She can go outside every day in our yard or on the playground, can walk in the park or ride down quiet roads in her stroller. Everyone knows her.

Hallowell, director of Laugh & Learn Preschool, is cheered by the babies.

"One of my favorite moments is when we have our weekly community coffee hour where people come and have coffee at Waterman's, and the toddlers come in and everybody's interacting and enjoying each other's company," she says. "It keeps the community vibrant and healthy."

Day, director of the Vinalhaven day-care center, agrees.

"It's great! I love it," she says. "I think it's wonderful to have so many kids on the island. It's great for the community, and we all work together to raise [our] kids." ♦

Courtney Naliboff lives, writes, teaches, and parents on North Haven. She writes a column for The Working Waterfront *and* Kveller.com, *and recently completed two manuscripts.*

Katie Johnson
Picturing Home

These images, all shot on Long Island in Casco Bay, are without a doubt my favorite collection of work, and closest to my heart.

It is important to me to provide a visual explanation of, and connection to, the place where I grew up. I am creating an ongoing body of work that not only documents the geography and culture of Long Island, but also provides insight into our community.

Growing up here, I had multiple sets of parents and grandparents, and many brothers and sisters. Until I left for college, I had never spent more than a week or so without seeing any of my island family.

Long Island is three miles long by one mile wide, and lies four miles off the coast. There are only five boats to the mainland a day, and just 230 people live here year-round. During the long winter months, *isolated* doesn't begin to describe what that feels like. But this community is full of intimate connections between the people and the land, the island's history, and with each other. Almost everyone is related, one way or another, and no one gets away with keeping any secrets. I have always feared change and the decline of this unique culture and society.

But it has been almost three years since the bulk of this portfolio was taken, and looking back through all the negatives in preparation for this publication, I see that not a lot has changed. Some of the people in the photos are no longer with us, and some have grown up. However, my fear of losing what makes life here special has been challenged, as I see sons become fathers, daughters marry into island life, and generation after generation succeed in preserving Long Island.

—Katie Johnson

REBECCA'S ROOM

MARSHALL

STEVIE & BILLINGS

HAZEL & NATALIE

HENRY & CAM

GRAMMY DAWN'S KITCHEN

BEACH AVE

VAL & MILLIE

A Fluent Blue

BY DOUGLAS W. MILLIKEN, WITH CAT BATES

A boy with a rowboat articulates his summer by ferrying tourists between two islands. From Monhegan's sandy beach bound by towering cliffs to the high grassy knuckle of Manana. Sculling over blue-green waves, he makes a fast five bucks each trip. And too, it's fun for him: What boy does not dream of captaining his own little ship at sea?

There is no uniformity to the tourists he ferries over. Some are solo, often men who grew up here on this toothy coast, whose lives have dictated they move somewhere far from home. Those are the quiet trips. There are families from distant cities, giddy and agog at the simple act of crossing above water in a paint-peeling wooden skiff. There are anxious young couples, eager to be alone on an unpeopled island. The boy takes them all. One family in particular, the boy remembers. A mother and father and very young daughter. Dressed too nice to be locals. Their accent an absence of accent. The family's plan is to take a leisurely walk through the high grassy dome of Manana while the boy waits for them by the slip, stretched out in the boat's belly and reading a book on mice. Everyone agrees: This is a good plan. Through the crossing, the mother is quiet and also looks tired, as if their vacation contains some built-in strain. The daughter is two maybe and mews like a cat: the indistinct sounds of an animal contented. The father, meanwhile, is a babbling cartoon, narrating their brief passage through the harbor like it's a sporting event, like a great moment in history. He shouts and gesticulates. He mistakes every buoy for a loon. For the boy, the crossing is the longest fifteen minutes of his life. For the mother, it likely feels longer.

What's clear is this: Throughout his own childhood, the father spent his summers on Monhegan. Running kites along the high cliffs. Watching for seals in the harbor. They've become a kind of dream-like jewel, his memories of Monhegan summers. And now he can share that jewel with his wife, with his daughter. This is his first return to the islands as an adult. His excitement boils over, over boils.

The boy does his best to suffer the man's exuberance in silence. It's obnoxious, he thinks, to so blatantly be a tourist, a summer person, a visitor. He has not quite realized: His relationship to this place might very well someday be identical to the man's.

From her pocket, the mother produces a hank of cloth, lightly dabs the sweat from her own and her daughter's face. The boy can tell: This kerchief was once part of a dress. Her husband points at a seagull and coos.

To distract himself from the sound and gestures of the father's unending monologue, the boy falls into meditating on the simple perfection of his old skiff's groaning oarlocks. There's the beauty of the object, sure, its gentle swoops almost like a horseshoe, both hard and masculine as a grappling fist yet elegant as the bell of a woman's swinging hips. But there is also the pure utility of the thing: Every aspect of its design is to accomplish a task and accomplish it well. Its beauty a by-product of its specialization. No ornament needed. It is perfect.

It's likely because of this adoring meditation that the boy loses one oarlock overboard. His attention is not on his task. Drawing the skiff alongside Manana's slip—at low tide, just a long ramp bearded in sea-moss and long ribbons of kelp—the boy raises the oars to stow beneath the bench seats, hears the splash of the popped-free lock, and too late knows exactly what he's lost.

An oarlock is designed to do one job well. Without it, that job is impossible.

The family, oblivious, clambers out onto the slip. The boy looks over the boat's flaking lip into the water's fluent blue. It's only maybe three feet deep here. But he cannot see bottom. So he cannot see the lock.

The boy knows he has time before he'll officially have stranded them out on Manana. While the family takes its long walk through the grass, he can dunk into the water, grasp at the sandy bottom, seek out what he has lost. But what if he cannot find the lock on his own? What if the family helps him? What if he asks them for help? The child, being a child, is both peripheral to and at the center of the problem—unable to assist, her presence raises the stakes— but what if the father finds the oarlock, redeeming his previous obnoxious behavior by becoming the hero of the day? What if it's the mother, tired, harried, the first-time visitor proving her dominion over this place?

What if no one finds it?

The boy looks from the disguising water to the family on the slip, reveals—in his posture, in his eyes—his embarrassment and danger and need. Up the slip, the upward tide lips. The family validates him by looking back.

If each moment is discrete and unrepeatable—is, by accomplishing itself just the one way, only ever meant to be that one way—does that mean each moment is perfect? Its form indistinguishable from its function. Executing its one job well.

If your job is to find: What do you find?

Four people row to an island, each seeking one thing but arriving at something else. ♦

Douglas W. Milliken is the author of four books, including the new pocket-sized collection, Cream River. *"A Fluent Blue" originally appeared as part of a multimedia jewelry/textile/text collaboration with the artist Cat Bates, whose own childhood experiences on Monhegan and Manana were instrumental in the writing of this story. You can learn more about that piece at cat-bates.com.*

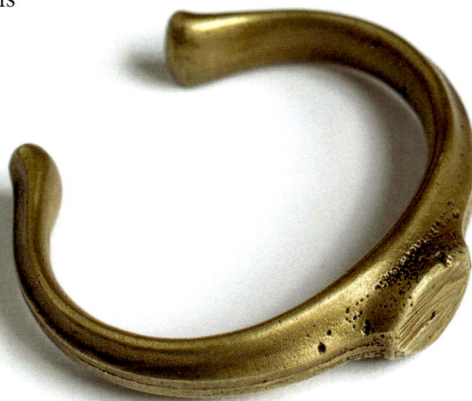

Victoria Smith and Cheabeague preschoolers listen to a story at Island Commons. JIM THRESHER

Not Aging, But *Thriving* in Place

Safe housing, health care for elderly pose challenges on islands

BY SUSAN Q. STRANAHAN

Victoria Smith was born on Chebeague Island on January 6, 1925, surrounded by her family in the neat frame home now occupied by her son and his wife. When she married an islander, they moved next door. Today, Smith's granddaughter, grandson-in-law, and two great-grandsons have a home nearby.

Three years ago, when Smith's health declined and living alone became difficult, she and her family made a choice available to few islanders: She moved about a mile away, into a cozy room at Chebeague's Island Commons, a seven-bed residential care home created for people exactly like Smith.

Lifelong friends live just down the hall at the Commons. Her extended family drops in daily. Friends stop by. She keeps tabs on the newest generation of Chebeaguers when students from the island's elementary school arrive for regular visits. Social events and workdays at the Commons attract the whole community. All the while, a team of trained caregivers works 24/7, helping with daily tasks, providing home-cooked meals and companionship, and overseeing the health and well-being of the elderly residents.

Smith is unstinting in her gratitude. "I feel Chebeague is truly blessed to have the Island Commons," she says.

• • •

Only recently has eldercare in Maine surfaced as a critical social and economic issue. Demographics drive that urgency. Maine has the highest percentage of older people in the United States, with a third of its population (nearly 420,000 people) above 55. That number will grow by 13 percent in just six years, according to a recent study. In

Elder Care Island Fellow Maddey Gates with Ivan Calderwood Home resident Maddy Hildings in a printmaking workshop using leaves collected from Vinalhaven.

pockets of the state, the median age already is considerably higher. On Chebeague, for example, it is 61, making the town the "grayest" of Maine's unbridged islands.

Age isn't the only statistic that makes eldercare a looming problem for government officials, nonprofit organizations, and policy makers. More than a third of Maine's population is considered low-income. Many of the state's elderly live in old houses, costly to maintain and heat, and often full of hazards for the frail or those with mobility problems. In rural communities, both on islands and the mainland, access to home care and even basic medical treatment is difficult and undependable, with transportation a major obstacle. Care often falls to family members, many ill-equipped financially or lacking in training.

And then there is the human side of the equation. Elders like Victoria Smith have spent their entire lives sustaining their small communities, raising families, supporting schools, churches, libraries, and volunteer organizations. In their final years, shouldn't they be able to live amid all that's familiar, close to family and friends? For many, that's simply not an option.

Twenty years ago, a small group of Chebeague residents, led by Charlotte "Pommy" Hatfield, recognized the lack of basic health-care services for islanders. Hatfield, a schoolteacher who had cared for her dying husband at home, had been rebuffed by mainland agencies and care providers unwilling to travel to the island. Unwilling to give up, Hatfield and her team came to a conclusion.

"We should do this ourselves," she recalled. "We knew nothing, but we just did it."

Hatfield researched what other regions of the country were doing, and familiarized herself with eldercare and hospice care requirements, eventually working as a care provider herself. What began as an effort to educate islanders about health and aging issues grew as the community members made clear what they wanted to have.

"They wanted comfort and care," said Hatfield. But there was more: "They wanted to see a familiar face."

Thus was born the Island Commons. Since it opened its doors in January 1999, the Commons has enabled more than 100 elders to "age in place," or, to borrow a more up-to-date term of care, "thrive in place."

An early document set out the ambitious goal: The Island Commons will be a "homey, congenial place where friends, relatives (including children), neighbors, and caregivers can drop in, lend a hand, or share a quiet moment." A 19th-century farmhouse was donated, renovations undertaken, and fund-raising began in earnest.

From the start, the challenges were enormous—and they remain just as daunting today. Nonstop fund-raising is essential simply to keep the Commons' doors open.

Typically, about two-thirds of Commons residents are MaineCare (Maine's name for its Medicaid program) recipients. Yet MaineCare reimbursement rates fail to cover the cost of delivering care by about $20,000 per person per year. And, given the small size of the facility and its remote location, even the most cost-conscious administrator is unable to achieve economies of scale available to larger mainland counterparts.

Facilities like the Commons also operate in a highly regulated environment, with rules governing everything

NANCY OLNEY

"They wanted comfort and care [and] they wanted to see a familiar face."

—Charlotte "Pommy" Hatfield

from the temperature of food in the refrigerator to the licensing of caregivers. Unlike other island nonprofits, the lights never go off at the Commons. Finding, training, and retaining staff to operate the facility round-the-clock can prove difficult.

But such challenges have not deterred other island communities from responding in their own ways to the needs of their elderly populations. Those services include the residential facilities Boardman Cottage on Islesboro and the Ivan Calderwood Home on Vinalhaven, with plans for a facility on North Haven in the works.

Maine Seacoast Mission, which has long provided health-care services in Penobscot Bay, is expanding its eldercare offerings. On Swan's Island, Eldercare Outreach offers a variety of services for elderly residents, intended to enable them to remain in their own homes for as long as possible. The Island Commons also recently added in-home care to its services through Chebeague Cares.

In many respects, this is new territory for health-care providers, regulators, volunteer board members, and facility administrators, in part because of the unique nature of each location and its needs. To share common experiences, an informal network of providers has formed to discuss problems and explore new services. (Many of the solutions being tried by island eldercare providers also have applications elsewhere, notably in Maine's rural and Native American communities.)

The island eldercare network also has demonstrated that there can be strength in numbers. Last year, the Maine Legislature approved a 15 percent increase in MaineCare subsidies for the Commons, Boardman Cottage, and Ivan Calderwood, recognizing that offshore locations drive up the cost of food and fuel, further straining the low subsidies. The increase came after testimony from island eldercare administrators about the importance of their services and their dire financial needs. The total outlay of state funds is small—about $26,000 annually—but the acknowledgment of the special circumstances was welcomed.

All who are involved in this growing response share a common goal: keeping island elders in their communities. "This is what they know," said Amy Rich, administrator at the Commons. "This is where their roots are, where their families are, and this is where they want to stay."

To make that possible, they may require modest services such as light housekeeping and meal preparation, or their needs might rise to the level of skilled nursing or hospice care. The advancing ages and declining health of many islanders pose their own set of challenges to the care providers that go far beyond the financial pressures of day-to-day operations.

• • •

It's late afternoon and Jen Belesca is sitting at her grandmother's bedside, massaging Victoria Smith's hands. The warm yellow bedroom, with chintz curtains and comfortable pillows, is full of family photos and mementos. From the hallway, the aroma of dinner fills the air.

Belesca stops in daily to keep "Grammy Toe," as Smith is known to her family, company. Belesca's sons, Ethan, 15, and Aaron, 14, often ride their bikes over to pay a call.

"She's right here," says Ethan of his great-grandmother. During last year's Fourth of July Road Race, he even stopped by to grab a glass of water and say "Hi" to her before resuming the race. Family members visit at meals and bedtime to assist Smith and keep her up-to-date on island news.

Those routine visits would be difficult if Smith were in a mainland nursing home. (Long before the Commons opened, Smith's own mother spent four years in a mainland nursing home, an experience the family never wants to repeat.) Now, Smith is just minutes away. The value of having her so close is apparent to everyone. "When the Commons came into being, it was one of the best things that ever happened to Chebeague," said her son, Lindy Smith. "I thought then it was a great idea—but I didn't realize how important it would become to this island." ♦

Susan Q. Stranahan lives on Chebeague Island and is president of the board of the Island Commons Resource Center. She is a veteran journalist, author of Susquehanna River of Dreams *and co-author of* Fukushima: The Story of a Nuclear Disaster.

Islands by the Numbers

23 — The number of cars the proposed replacement ferry for the Bass Harbor to Swan's Island run would be able to carry. The current ferry, the *HENRY LEE*, carries 17 cars. The new ferry is slated to go online in 2020.

105 — The number of deer killed and "tagged" on Islesboro in the 2015 expanded archery-only hunt.

756,664 — The number of tickets sold for Peaks Island by the Casco Bay Lines in 2015.

$275,567 — Median house price on North Haven. Maine's median house price is $180,000.

9.5 million — The number of pounds of lobster landed in Vinalhaven in 2015; the value of the catch there was $39 million.

10,520,000 — Kilowatt hours produced in 2015 by the Fox Islands Wind turbines; Vinalhaven and North Haven used 9.9 million kilowatt hours.

4 — The number of students in the school on Cliff Island.

9 — The number of students expected to graduate from Islesboro Central School in 2016.

66,000 — The number of gallons of diesel used to generate electricity on Monhegan Island (31,000 gallons) and Matinicus Island (35,000 gallons) in 2014.

0 — The number of six-packs of beer sold at The Island Market and Supply store on Swan's Island in 2015. The sale of alcohol is not legal on the island.

$12,000–$15,000 — The amount of money raised annually through bottle and can redemption on Vinalhaven for the island's senior housing facility.

3 — The number of golf courses on Maine islands (Islesboro, North Haven, and Chebeague).

9 — The number of active lobstermen operating from Monhegan.

ART BY ALEXIS IAMMARINO

A TALE TO TELL

Phippsburg's Eugene Atwood faced three near-death experiences on the water

He's known around the peninsula below Bath as Captain Bullhead. The stubborn will the nickname implies may have saved his life. Now 75, Eugene Atwood survived three serious threats to his life, served up by the sea and from trying to wrest a living from it. The last, about 12 years ago, was the most dramatic.

"They always say the third time never fails, but Christ, I think I got by it," he says.

Was it divine intervention that saved him?

"No, I don't believe in that stuff. I might as well say that up front. I believe in what I can do."

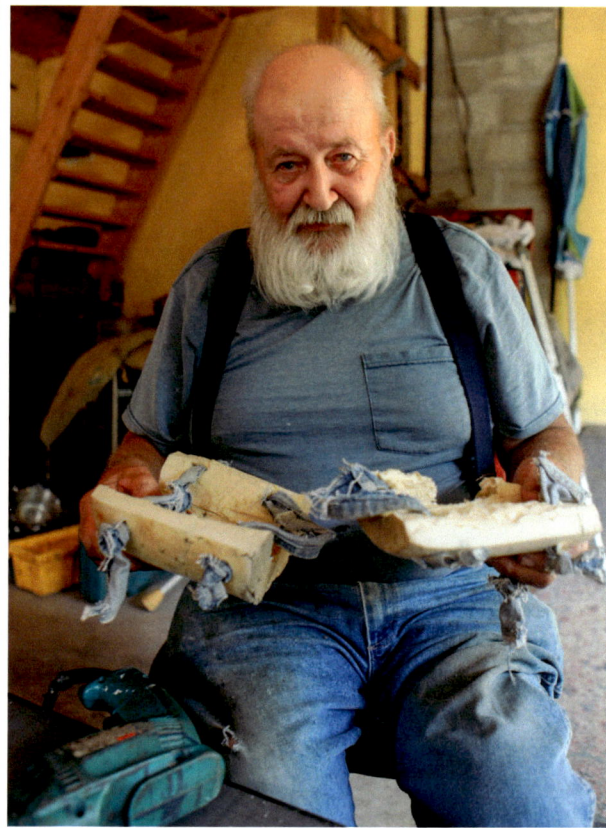

Eugene Atwood with his "sandals" SCOTT SELL

I was born in Bath. I was working down on the wharf when I was 14.

The first of it, I fished for lobster, then I got a dragger. I've had about three draggers.

The first thing that happened, years ago, we dragged up a depth charge. We tied it on the deck, and [people from the Brunswick Naval] air base came over and got it, and they said if we'd throwed it overboard it might've gone off, 'cause it was all set for a certain depth. They said we were just lucky it didn't go off. We didn't know what it was. We tied it off because it was rolling around the deck. It was a great big round one.

After my helper cleaned it off, it said "depth charge" right on it. That was the first lucky one.

The next one was, my daughter and I was in the boat that burned. It was around 1977. I think it was a 19- or 20-foot Seaworthy. What happened, the hauling motor run out of gas, so I took the can and went up and when I tipped up and started filling it, the gas, I guess, went on the manifold or something, and it went off, and I dropped the can, and when I did it went on me and then it rolled back and went on my daughter. She was out there baiting a trap.

I went right out over the outboard, and she jumped right overboard, too, because the boat went on fire.

We had oil clothes on and we couldn't hardly swim. There was a trap buoy got caught on the outboard—the boat was going away from us—so we got ahold of it then, because it stopped. That was the lucky part.

If it hadn't been for that, we'd probably drowned.

It burned the inside and almost down to the waterline on the other side. It still floated. There was a Mrs. Cushman, I think it was, who owned Burnt Coat Island, they was painting a float and her and a little kid come out and got us. They was watching us. We lucked out pretty good.

[The third time] it was the summertime. We were setting traps. It was probably around 8, 9 o'clock. It was kind of a pleasure boat, but it was all cut down, and ripped out, like a flat-bottomed skiff. About 16-foot. Carrying 24 traps, something like that, on it.

Something happened up in the bow, 'cause I was going right along, and then I see water come up around my feet, just a little bit at a time, so I slowed her down, and when I did, it tipped right up on the bow. And I think what happened, she must have cracked up in the bow. When I slowed down, then she tipped up. And when she did, she went. And all the floating rope come up and kind of got ahold of me, and I had fun then.

I tried to get that off the top of me, it was sawing into my neck and everything else. That was kind of scary, then, but I guess you're just too busy getting it off you. You're just trying to survive. The only thing on your mind is getting on top of that water and breathing. I got out of it, come up, gagging, spitting water, all that stuff. All I can remember is bubbles. I was just trying to stay afloat, 'cause I had boots on. Christ, you could kick, but it don't do any good.

Some buoys floated up—two or three buoys—and I got one, and that helped me float a little bit, and I got another one, and put one under each arm and it was just like a life preserver. Then my dinner bucket come up. It was one of them Igloos. I sat it up straight, and kept pushing it ahead of me and swam in towards the island, about a quarter of a mile away. I did think if there was any sharks; that did cross my mind. It probably does everybody. They've seen sharks up in there.

I had a little job getting up on the island, 'cause the breakers were coming in. I went up once, and went back down. Christ, my dinner bucket went right in and set right up. The second time, I went up. It was hard on my fingers,

though, trying to get ahold of them rocks, and you'd slide down across there.

Then I got up on the rocks, and Granville Wallace was hauling traps. It was foggy—it was right thick—I could just see him. I hollered, but he couldn't hear me, with the boat running and everything. So I just took off, walking. It's quite big . . . Big Wood Island. There's probably three or four houses on it now. There's one on a cove up on the north end, that's where I was headed for.

I found a buoy and made me a pair of shoes. I took my jackknife out and split the trap buoy. Then I cut the bottom of my pants off [into strips] and made little sandals, 'cause there was all rocks going up across there. There was kind of a high cliff, then it was all bushes and then it went up into the trees and woods. But I stayed down on the edge and went along the rocks.

And when I got up to the cottage, I went around and on the back side, they left a window unlocked. So I went in and got me a pair of sandals—women's slippers, with fur all around the top—a flashlight, and got me some bug spray… everything I needed. It was getting late then. I was on the island all day. It took a long time to climb them rocks. There was a lot of big rocks, cliffs. I had to go down on my knees and climb. I couldn't go very fast.

Keith Wallace was out hunting for me. He was in his big boat, and he come around the shore, and I kept flashing my light and he come in as close as he could. And he went clear home, and got his skiff and come back in. Then he rowed in and got me. It must have been 8:30.

My skiff and outboard, nobody ever got it. I don't know why. I set traps, right on top of where I was. I guess somebody probably got it and didn't say nothing.

It worked out good. Christ, it was just another day. I thought about it [later], but it was nothing to worry you. Just another day, I guess. If you were to have panicked, why, then, Christ, you'd probably have killed yourself.

You know, there's some people get drowned and some people come out of it. But that's something they learn when they're doing it, I guess. I don't think it's anything you can prevent. If it's going to happen, it's going to happen. That's why they call it an "accident." ♦

Big Wood Island SCOTT SELL

ME 124 TH

PATRICIA ANN
CHEBEAGUE ISLAND, ME

RACE DAY IN CASCO BAY

Lobstermen blow off steam—but hopefully, not their engines—in boat-racing circuit

BY TOM GROENING
PHOTOS BY KATIE JOHNSON

> "This is the perfect mix between family reunion and tractor pull."
>
> —Travis Otis

George Ross enjoys the best seat in the house for the race.

I'm squatting in the small cockpit of an outboard-powered sailboat racing across Casco Bay. Lightning bolts are striking the mainland and islands to our west. I look up at the aluminum mast, then at the woman at the wheel. She's wearing a wide grin and a purple feather boa.

Everything is going to be just fine, I think. After all, what could go wrong when lightning and sailboat masts come together?

Then my hat flies off.

But I'm grinning, too, even though the rooster tail churned up by the twin, 250-horsepower outboards is lapping over the rail, soaking my pants.

As discordant as these elements might seem, they are, in fact, entirely appropriate for the sometimes wacky, sometimes wild, and always fun world of lobster-boat races. This hot and humid August Saturday, it was Long Island's turn to host the contest. The race circuit is a summer tradition in Maine, with towns and harbors hosting the events from Jonesport and Beals Island in the northeast all the way to Long Island in the southwest.

The Long Island races this year lean toward the wacky end of the spectrum, in part because there were no cash prizes for winners. The sailboat I raced in, aptly named WILD WOMEN, was actually the top half of a sailboat that had been attached to the hull of a powerboat. We raced—and won—in an "anything goes" class. The only thing the hybrid boat had in common with the others in that heat was that all had been built by Steve Johnson, who owns and operates Johnson's Boatyard on the island.

Johnson was at Sandie Moran's side—the feather boa–wearing woman who piloted WILD WOMEN—when the boat won that final heat of the day. It ended up being the final heat because the Coast Guard contacted race organizers and said the lightning was headed our way, and it was time to end the fun and be safe.

The two were clearly enjoying the afterglow of their victory, suggesting that even with all the goofy trappings of the race, a competitive edge runs through the event.

In other harbors, the races are very competitive because of the prizes, and, of course, because bragging rights are at stake. This, the 2015 race, was the second year the Long Island event has counted in the points totals. As one participant explained, it's very much like NASCAR, with racers racking up points through the summer.

HARD WORK, THEN FUN

Earlier in the day, making the rounds on the docks and town landing as observers and participants gathered, the race seemed like the island version of a county fair. At about 11 a.m., Moran was stocking coolers with beer on WILD WOMEN, but that chore was the last of many.

"It's an awful lot of work, organizing it," she said of the race. "Keeping it going is a challenge."

Why do it?

"So these guys who work so hard can cut loose," she says.

That explanation is repeated by many. Though most fishermen will tell you they love being their own boss, love being out in the elements, lobstering is solitary, repetitive work. Hanging out with other fishermen, on the water, talking boats and engines, and yes, drinking beer, is a nice way to break up that solitude.

Travis Otis and his father, Keith, of Searsport, build lobster boats—the Northern Bay 36-foot among them—and were on hand to race. Their boat, FIRST TEAM, named for the unit Keith served with in Vietnam, features a 410-horsepower diesel engine, and will compete with like-size boats.

"This is my family reunion," Keith says. "We've been racing for 15 years, so I know all these jokers," he adds, gesturing to the boats docked adjacent to his.

Travis offers what is the best description of the race scene: "This is the perfect mix between family reunion and tractor pull."

How serious does the Otis family take these races?

"Pretty seriously," Travis says, cocking his head and smiling. They've won their class seven years running.

Chris Smith of Richmond, a town up the Kennebec River, uses his boat MISTY, a 33-foot Crowley, to chase eels, the adult versions of elvers. It's his eighth year on the race circuit.

"You get to travel up and down the coast and meet nice people," he says, an observation his wife Linda seconds.

The blind-folded dinghy races

Lee MacVane, in his 30s, is originally from Long Island but now lives in and fishes from Cape Elizabeth. This is the only race he's doing, running his 46-foot, 670-horsepower boat, aptly called DOMINATOR. "I don't know," he says, thinking about why he participates in the race. "It's just a good chance to get out and unwind, and see people you don't normally get to see."

Bill Randall of Hiram is a summer resident of Long Island.

"I'm here with my grandson Preston and my son Ryan," he says proudly.

"This is a fun event. It's a good time; they got good eats."

John Murphy of Portland is a summer resident of the island—a "summer dub," as he calls himself, though his family has been coming here for five generations—and he loves the event.

"A lot of these people work really hard," he says, repeating the refrain. "It's their way of having a good time."

Before the races begin, there are shoreside events, like a dinghy race in which the rower is blindfolded and directed by the other occupant of the boat. There's also a race in which participants swim in those bulky survival suits.

A band plays in the parking lot and hot dogs and burgers are being grilled, with sale proceeds going to the island fire and rescue department.

RAFTING UP

Out on the water, the real fun begins. Katie Johnson, the photographer for this story, is an island native, and she gets us aboard her stepfather Scott Wood's boat, WILD ONE. In a matter of minutes, three, five, and then eight boats have tied up, side to side, in what is known as "rafting up." The coolers open, food and beer is passed around, and people climb from boat to boat, greeting old friends, shaking hands with new ones, and taking photos. Teen

girls in bikinis on the boat to one side of us leap into the water to cool off, as does a dog.

When it's time for a boat to race, it's untied and the other vessels close ranks, as if the racing boat had never been there.

On the radio, there's evidence that racers have jumped the gun: "I think we're going to have to do the second race again."

This prompts a comment from Randy Durkee, who's come down from Islesboro to race BLACK DIAMOND, tied next to us: "Jesus Christ, they ain't got it figured out yet?"

When it's time for WILD ONE to race, everyone leaves the boat, except for Wood at the helm, Katie and I, and George Ross, who visits the island every summer from Marietta, Georgia, and loves the races. The engine cover is lifted off as we chug over and join a handful of boats, lined up along a vague line in the water. When the start signal comes by radio, the engine roars and the boat lurches forward.

Within a minute, black smoke is coming off the engine block, Katie is bouncing around the deck, shooting photos, and George sits motionless in a chair near the stern, a grin that seems to have been carved into his face his only reaction. A minute later, it's clear we won't win, as one vessel pulls away.

> # "It's just a good chance to get out and unwind, and see people you don't normally get to see."
>
> ## —Lee MacVane

Back with the other boats, the fun resumes. We've got the best seat in the house to see the finishes, and corresponding to friendships with fishermen, there's loud rooting for one or another boat.

Jennifer Franz, who with her husband Rick lives on nearby Great Diamond Island, is among the folks aboard WILD ONE. She tells the story of being on a racing boat several years back: As the race got under way, the captain looked over at a competitor's boat.

"He's cheating!" the lobsterman shouted.

"How do you know?" she asked.

"Because I'm cheating," he replied. "And goddamn it, he's beating us!"

Cheating—if there is any—could be achieved by introducing fuel additives or modifying the engine.

Franz tells another story that sums up the lobster boat–race vibe. It was one of the first years she and Rick were on a racing boat, and when that boat was readying to race, she asked if she should move her bags and cooler to a non-racing boat so the racer would be lighter.

An older woman said, in a sweet and motherly voice, "You do whatever suits you, dear." The sentiment, Franz says, is that having fun is paramount here.

Jennifer and Rick visit Long Island often, and though they are not a fishing family—they own and operate Andy's Old Port Pub on Commercial Street in Portland, a sponsor of the race—many of the fishermen know the couple and exchange good-natured banter with them.

Copious amounts of alcohol are consumed throughout the day, but it seems to be mostly festive fun. Joe Schnapp, the island deputy, was out and about, patrolling the shore, but he was all smiles and hellos, walking among the crowd.

"It's a wonderful time. It's a good community event," he says.

And when the Coast Guard radios organizers to pull the plug in deference to the lightning, the deputy's take seems like the right way to sum up the day. ♦

Tom Groening is editor of Island Journal.

Race day is a family affair: children attack another boat with their water guns.

There is a magical quality to living in Maine. And we're proud to make magic happen for our clients.

PHOTO: BRIAN VANDEN BRINK

Phi
HOME DESIGNS

446 WEST STREET, ROCKPORT, MAINE 04856 | 207.230.0034

ARCHITECTS · BUILDERS · CABINET & FURNITURE MAKERS

phihomedesigns.com

Twice to the Island for Islesboro Teacher Jon Bolduc

Raised on the island, he returned to teach

BY TOM GROENING

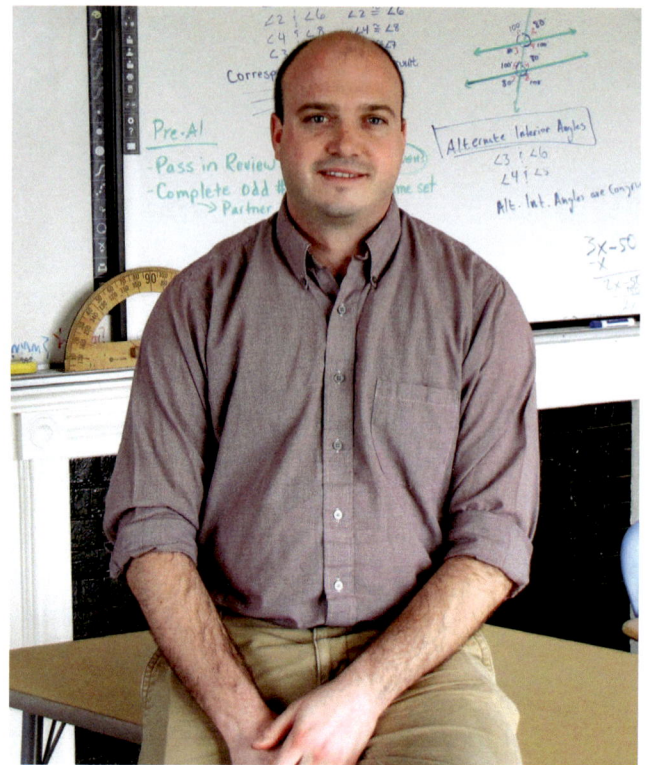

TOM GROENING

Islesboro has a personal and professional hold on Jon Bolduc, and for good reason, as he explains. Bolduc, 31, moved with his family to the Penobscot Bay island when he was a child.

"My mom and dad were both teachers," he explains. "They got positions the same year" at the Islesboro Central School. "We moved out in 1990, my two sisters and I. I was going into kindergarten then."

Bolduc graduated from the island school in 2003 and then went to college at the University of Maine at Farmington. He taught at Carrabec High School in North Anson, near Skowhegan, for four years.

"This will be my fourth year teaching here," he said.

IJ: This school is unusual in that it draws mainland students, and its reputation is excellent, but I wonder: Are there any drawbacks, educationally—and you can speak to this personally or professionally—growing up on an island?

Bolduc: There are drawbacks, obviously, with small class sizes and a small community. As a student, sometimes our options can be limited, both socially and maybe athletically. We have a soccer team, but that's it, for the fall. We have a basketball team, but that's it for the winter. On the flip side of that, it could be a good thing: Because we are so small, we can create opportunities with different pathways for students. Right now, we have a kid working with Dark Harbor Boat Yard on 700 Acre Island. Every other day, he's out there, working with them. It's kind of an internship. He's a sophomore, and has been really interested in boats.

There are those opportunities that arise with such a small school. You can really focus on the individual, and it's difficult for them to slip through the cracks, which is great.

Socially, as a teenager, you're going to have fights with your friends, but you have to make it work, because there's nobody else. That's kind of a good, lifelong skill that I've always taken away from it. You have disagreements, you've got to work them out, which is a life skill.

IJ: You teach math. And your wife also teaches here?

Bolduc: She does. She's a K-through-one teacher. Both of these positions opened up the same year, so we moved out here.

IJ: Are there particular challenges to teaching math to kids? Maybe not so much on Islesboro, but on islands like Vinalhaven, many of the kids want to go and fish. What are the challenges you face in making math relevant to your students?

Bolduc: Trying to fulfill each individual student's needs is probably the greatest challenge of a teacher. Just trying to differentiate one lesson, trying to teach it three or four different ways for three or four different levels, trying to challenge the students that are really understanding it, but still working with those kids that are struggling to understand the concepts—that's one of the hardest things to do.

I teach everything from pre-algebra all the way up to calculus. It's a lot of different subject matter. I was a math major in college; I can handle that pretty easily. But within the classroom, even though there are small classes—ten students is a big class here—among those ten students, you're going to have such a wide range.

But at the same time, you have so much individual time with them—maybe not during class, but built into the schedule. We have this "academy time," where they can come meet with you, so it's a lot of one-on-one, which is great.

IJ: Okay, a more personal question: Are you an extrovert or an introvert, and how does island life fit your personality type?

Bolduc: I'm an introvert, which is good and bad. On the island, you can easily do nothing, sit at home, and be fine. But that's not the lifestyle I want to live.

This community's very supportive. I don't feel out of place. I'm an introvert, but I like to go and do things, but . . . I guess I'm reserved.

I would much rather hike around Turtle Head than go to the mall or the club.

IJ: How much interaction do you have with summer folks?

Bolduc: A fair amount. Growing up, I had a lot of interaction, because I worked at the golf course. My summer job now is landscaping, so I've worked for a couple of summer folks doing that.

I've also done some tutoring of summer kids.

Even with the summer community, it's pretty close-knit. You run into them at the store and talk to them. For the most part, they're all very accessible. I know they do a lot for the school, so that's nice.

IJ: Have you ever met summer residents John Travolta or Kirstie Alley?

Bolduc: Yeah. I haven't really "met" John Travolta. I saw him once in the Dark Harbor Shop; he shook my hand. I don't know why, but he did [laughs]. He just looked at me and said, "Hi!"

Kirstie Alley . . . Growing up, my older sister used to go over and [Kirstie] would do her and her friends' hair and makeup, and dress them up. She used to come to basketball games. She was really involved in the community.

My parents were building our house, and we had to get out of the house we were living in, and so we were living in a tent in the backyard. And of course, in the summer, it was rainy . . . She just came by one day and threw us the keys to her guesthouse that's up by the ball field, which she had at the time, and said, "Stay as long as you want!"

And so my whole family got to live there; that's just the type of person she was. She's not around as much as she used to be. She was very generous.

IJ: Do you think about whether your young daughter would come back to the island, or is that too far off to think about?

Bolduc: I think that's too far off. I'm not going to push that on her either way. Whatever she wants. I think it's going to be a great place for her to grow up. From there, we'll see. Maybe she'll become a lobsterman, I don't know [laughs].

IJ: There's no real real downtown, village center here. Does that inhibit community cooperation, or . . . ?

Bolduc: I always thought it would be neat to have that kind of downtown, like when you go to North Haven and Vinalhaven. But I don't think I really miss that aspect. I don't think it hurts the community spirit at all. There's a fair amount of collaboration, cooperation. There's the Islesboro Community Center, which was built six years ago. They do a lot of great things, a lot of summer programs.

I laugh when people come over on the ferry in the summer and they're walking and they ask where to go. They're not going to make it very far.

IJ: Last question: Do you ever think about moving off-island?

Bolduc: Yes. And I don't think I want to. We moved out here just to give it a try. We both moved here because of the dream scenario, the dream positions. We had talked about it, [my wife] Becky and I, but we knew it wouldn't happen unless two positions opened in the same year, and that happened.

We really enjoy the school. I love the community. And I couldn't ask to teach any better kids. So considering moving off, I have a really hard time thinking about wanting to teach anywhere else.

A teacher asked me that question, and my answer was, "I wouldn't be a teacher if I moved off." And what the heck else would I do? ♦

Widow's Island:
A Curious Tale of Quarantine and Convalescence

Yellow fever, mental illness, and war wounds treated on island off North Haven

BY CARL LITTLE // PHOTOS BY WILLIAM TREVASKIS

B ack in the 1970s when I lived on Long Island, New York, I had occasion to take the ferry from Orient Point to New London. I remember passing Plum Island and being told there was a center for disease research on it. Visions of infected patients wandering the island gave me the creeps. In fact, the facility, founded in 1954 and now under the aegis of Homeland Security, has focused on the study of foot-and-mouth disease in cattle. Area residents have never fully embraced its existence, and have even come up with a theory that Lyme disease was created there as a biological weapon, but escaped the island. Seagoing folk passing by Widow's Island in the late 1800s might have gotten similar vibes. This 15-acre isle off the eastern shore of North Haven, one of several flanking the Fox Islands Thoroughfare, was home to a quarantine station built by the US Navy to house sailors returning from foreign ports, Panama in particular, who had contracted yellow fever.

Why Widow's? Colder climates were thought to aid in the recovery from the deadly virus, which is transmitted by infected mosquitoes, a fact doctors didn't know at the time. With the quarantine station in Portsmouth, New Hampshire, "antiquated and played out," this island seemed like a perfect spot to isolate victims while they recovered.

So the US Navy had procured Widow's and built a temporary hospital—a pavilion—in 1885, and then, in 1888, a permanent facility, an imposing two-story brick building that could accommodate fifty patients. Both structures were built by W. H. Glover & Co. of Rockland.

Area citizens were none too pleased to have this possible source of contagion in their backyard; a "remonstrance" expressing their concerns was circulated on North Haven and Vinalhaven in 1885. The *Courier-Gazette* of May 12 of that year stated, "The people in the vicinity have no cause for alarm," noting that at Portsmouth, "rusticators have built their cottages right down to the quarantine line, and have no fear of contagious diseases, [even] though two yellow fever vessels were anchored there last year."

Dr. A. C. Heffinger, the naval surgeon put in charge of the project, helped sell the idea, inviting "leading citizens" of Rockland to the island for tours of the facility. In the end, they needn't have worried. The complex never actually housed any yellow fever patients, thanks to new knowledge about the malady.

A bit of history: In his *Islands of the Mid-Maine Coast: Blue Hill and Penobscot Bays* (1983), Charles McLane offered an account of the island's habitation. Originally called Sheep Island on John Vinal's map of the area, Widow's was a part of the Winslow Farm on North Haven, its *Addams Family*-esque name honoring Josiah Winslow's wife, who spent nearly a half-century in widowhood.

Deemed unnecessary as a quarantine station, on January 1, 1904, the facility was transferred by the US government to the State of Maine to be used as a summer retreat for the "convalescent insane." For the next ten years, local islanders witnessed the comings and goings of groups of men and women from the Maine Insane Asylum in Augusta and Bangor.

In an article in the *Courier-Gazette* from fall 1971, Rockland resident Albert Mills Sr. shared memories of the facility from when he worked there during the summers of 1909 and 1910. By this time,

the island's name had been changed to Chase's, in honor of Judge Edward Everett Chase of Blue Hill. According to McLane, it was Chase, a trustee of the Maine State Mental Hospitals, who had urged the transfer of the Widow's Island hospital to the state. The facility came to be called the Chase Island Convalescent Hospital.

The son of the keeper of nearby Goose Rocks Light, Mills had been hired by Manning S. Campbell, treasurer of the Maine State Hospital, to be the on-site engineer. With help from the keeper, Captain Frank Cooper, he took care of the water and electricity, no mean feat in this remote outpost. He also serviced the boats, which included the WHIM, a small open launch, and the 40-foot schooner GENERAL KNOX, which carried patients and personnel on cruises around the islands. In that 1971 article, Mills described a picnic on Vinalhaven during which a female patient disappeared and was found hours later at the North Haven post office.

Mills described the grounds, which featured trees planted in 1885 by officers of the 127-ton naval tugboat ROCKET, in order to make the property less destitute. (In photos of the era, only a few spruce trees accent the sheep-shorn island; today, it is more or less covered in evergreens.) A large swimming pool built near the shore could be filled with seawater at high tide and then shut off to be warmed by

The hospital, ca. 1888
(Courtesy North Haven Historical Society)

the sun. "It gave the patients a nice change and [a] summer vacation," Mills wrote.

Reading excerpts from the diaries of Dr. Bigelow Sanborn (1839–1910), physician at, and then superintendent of, the Maine Insane Asylum from 1866 until his death, one realizes that the challenges of dealing with mental illness in Maine go back generations. Transcribed by Sanborn's granddaughter, Margaret Hodgdon, the diary mentions issues familiar to anyone following the current tribulations of the Department of Health and Human Services: lack of funding, deferred maintenance, a sometimes stingy legislature, and a scrutinizing press.

There are touches of *Cider House Rules* in Dr. Sanborn's reports. Outbreaks of diphtheria and *la grippe*, snowstorms, residents setting fire to beds, physicians abusing alcohol and morphine—the accounts are matter-of-fact but often startling. Not all is disaster control: The Togus minstrels and the Augusta Brass Band performed for the patients, and there were magic lantern shows and picnics.

The name "Widows Island" (without the apostrophe) appears for the first time in entries for 1905. Following a visit by Dr. Sanborn, his wife, and hospital trustees to inspect the facility, the Maine Insane Asylum began taking patients to the island in the summer and fall.

"On August 4," the superintendent reported, "I went down to Widows Island with 28 females and took back the males." Dr. Sanborn noted the mostly positive impact of this retreat in his diary. He already knew the beneficial effects of a Maine island on patients: In the 1890s he organized annual trips by steamboat to his summer home on the Isle of Springs. When "Mr. Chase's experiment" closed

in 1915, historian McLane recounted, the facility was for a short time repurposed as a school for the children of lighthouse keepers. During World War I, US Navy sailors came to the island to convalesce from injuries and illness.

The hospital was torn down in 1935 "as a WPA project." An April 1986 article in *Down East* magazine, with the somewhat sensational title "Widow Island's Tainted Past," noted that the bricks from the building "found their way into fireplaces on nearby Vinalhaven, and the rest were used to weight lobster traps in Penobscot Bay." The island became a bird sanctuary, and then, writes McLane, the summer home "of a vacationing realtor."

A fitting finale to this curious piece of Maine island history might be the last stanza from Mary W. Litchfield's poem, "Governor's Day at Widow's Island," written on September 5, 1905, and inspired by the visit of former Maine governor Frederick Robie and other dignitaries, including Judge Chase, to the island. As the sunset lights up the Camden Hills and drives "grief and gloom away,"

All too soon the party leaves us,
Pleasant guests, though short their stay,
Long by us will be remembered
Widow's Island's gala day. ♦

(Thanks to Jason Mann, and to Nan Lee, John Storck, and Kate Quinn at the North Haven Library and Historical Society, for providing background and photographs.)

Carl Little is co-author with his brother David of the forthcoming Art of Acadia (Down East Books). He lives and writes on Mount Desert Island.

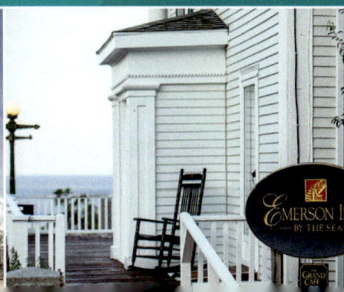

The morning light from Kirkjufellsfoss, Western Island

Fire & Ice

Iceland's Stark Beauty Found Outside Reykjavík on Ring Road

PHOTOS AND STORY BY JLYNN FRAZIER

Maine's connections to the North Atlantic island nation of Iceland are stronger than you might think. Eimskip—Iceland's oldest shipping company, which operates around the globe—is based in Reykjavík. Portland is Eimskip's only US-based port. Last fall, a delegation from Iceland visited Portland to discuss how to boost cultural connections between Reykjavík and Portland.

Also in the fall, my partner Jared and I headed to Iceland for a two-week road trip.

Reykjavík, the capital, is where two-thirds of the nation's population of 329,100 lives. To put it in perspective, Maine has four times as many residents living in roughly a third of the land mass. Reykjavík served as our starting and ending point to stock up on supplies, but for most of the trip, we explored the wilds of the rural landscape that makes up so much of the country.

Our mission was to circumnavigate the island by traveling the 1,332-kilometer (828-mile) coastal route known as the Ring Road. The route was completed in 1974 and consists of two lanes, one going in each direction, with many small, one-lane bridges made out of wood or steel. Most of the road is paved, though many sections are still gravel.

We found that as we detoured off the Ring Road and started inland, the roads quickly became very challenging. They label them accordingly as "F" roads to signify that four-wheel drive is required. We pushed the little two-wheel-drive camper van we had rented past its limits, but still managed several successful adventures off the beaten path. We were forced to cut short a couple of adventures when roads were rendered impassable by loose sand or deep water. Lesson learned: Iceland adventures require four-wheel drive.

We didn't set a concrete itinerary, opting instead to use a Lonely Planet guide and plan the details on the fly from our camper van, allowing us the flexibility to experience anything the island might have to offer us that day.

On the morning of our first full day, we were greeted with a fresh blanket of snow, then further welcomed by the high winds and torrential rains that were the remnants of Hurricane Joaquin. Then it rained, and rained some more.

In fact, these were some of the heaviest rains we had ever experienced. It turns out the "Land of Fire and Ice," as Iceland is known, also can be the land of brutal and unpredictable weather. So with the weather report grimly forecasting no end in sight to the rain, we grudgingly abandoned the southern reaches of the island and spent an entire day on the road, driving east toward the hope of blue skies and our first view of the fjords.

We continued our way around the Ring Road, occasionally making detours to explore remote areas like Þingvellir National Park and the Westfjords, venturing down rough dirt roads and across mountain passes to catch glimpses of snowcapped volcanoes, hidden waterfalls, and imposing glaciers. We saw a lot of sheep grazing in fields, and sometimes crossing the road in front of us. There are many more sheep than people, according to my research.

Being there outside of peak tourist season, which is June to August, meant we could often spend an entire day driving without seeing another person. The few people we did interact with were exceptionally friendly and welcoming.

I remember one early morning waiting for the only gas station in town to open so that we could get a cup of coffee. The coffee came in small, eight-ounce cups. The owner chuckled as we both approached the counter with two cups in each of our hands. "Ah," he said. "Americans always want more coffee."

Another morning we arrived at the small fishing town of Hólmavík (pop. 337), again looking for hot beverages, breakfast, and much-needed diesel. We pulled into the petrol station next to a local man refueling his truck. As Jared began to pump, the man greeted him, saying, "Isn't life beautiful? And it just keeps getting better and better each day, doesn't it?"

Jared, not yet properly caffeinated, replied, "Yes, I suppose it does." The man grinned, hopped in his truck, and went off to enjoy the rest of his day.

Such a simple statement, yet so powerful. Yes, it was a beautiful day, and we felt so fortunate that Iceland had welcomed us so warmly. ♦

Jlynn Frazier is the Island Institute's membership manager.

To view more of Jlynn's photography, visit her website at www.jfrazierphotography.com.

Loftsalahellir, a cave used for council meetings during the Saga times, is located just before the causeway to Dyrhólaey, Southwest Iceland.

Trading Sardines for Lupines

Eastport's rebirth may portend a new kind of rejuvenation

BY ROB MCCALL

The sardine—a generic name for several types of herring—is the icon of Eastport, which likes to call itself "the easternmost city in the USA." Eastport encompasses five islands, the largest being Moose Island. With a population of only about 1,300 people, Eastport still remembers its heritage every New Year's Eve by dropping, not a sparkling ball, but a giant sardine from the roof of the tallest building on Water Street.

At its peak, Eastport had 5,000 people and dozens of sardine canneries in operation when the herring were running, and Eastport sardines were shipped around the world. We first came to Eastport in the mid-1970s, camping out on Cobscook Bay. We built a cabin on Leighton Neck in 1980. When I was called to serve as pastor of the Congregational Church in Blue Hill in 1986, one of the many enticements—along with fields of lupine—was that our camp was just a two-hour drive away. In the fall of 2014,

we moved to Eastport to live there year-round, just in time for the coldest and snowiest winter ever recorded in the state. The golden age for Eastport ended in the 1950s as the herring dwindled, the canneries began to close down, and the city slipped into a depression, both economically and emotionally. There were few bleaker places along the Maine coast. In the 1970s, Tim Sample joked about an Eastport "Vacant Building Festival," and quipped that if you could buy a Greyhound bus ticket with food stamps, there would be no one left in town. He could have said the same about most of Washington County.

• • •

Washington County's population in 2010 was 32,856; the estimate for 2014 was 31,808, showing a decline of 3.2 percent. At 3,255 square miles, of which 695 square miles

LESLIE BOWMAN

A side street in Eastport TOM GROENING

are water, the county is a good deal larger than Delaware. Due to the Native American population and a surprising number of Hispanic settlers who came to rake blueberries and stayed, the minority population is almost 10 percent, compared to about 6 percent for the rest of Maine, and less than 4 percent for neighboring Hancock County.

There are many conservation lands, notably Moosehorn National Wildlife Refuge, at over 28,000 acres; Cobscook Bay State Park, at 888 acres; and Quoddy Head State Park, at 541 acres, where you can hear the grumbling of softball-size rocks being rolled up and down the beach by wind and waves coming up the Grand Manan Channel.

Economically, about 20 percent of the people in the Sunrise County are living below the federal poverty line, compared to about 14 percent in Maine as a whole. According to Good Shepherd Food Bank, Washington County has a food insecurity rate of 17.6 percent, and 28 percent of county children regularly face hunger. Unemployment in 2013 was 7.7 percent, compared to 5.1 percent for the state. The suicide rate is 16.7 percent per 100,000, the third-highest in the state.

• • •

Not long ago, I pulled into a gas station mini-mart way Downeast on Route 1 for a cup of coffee and a blueberry muffin. I parked next to an older, banged-up Dodge Ram pickup, covered with a coating of oil and dust. In the bed were rubber boots, a chain saw, some plastic fish totes, and numerous rusting tools—nothing unusual here, where the pickup trucks still outnumber the Subarus by about two to one.

What caught my eye was the vinyl lettering on the back window which read, "In Loving Memory of Lillian —————, 1975–2015," with a photo beneath showing a haggard woman who could easily have been 65. With a bit of a shock, I said to myself, "I know her."

She used to call on the church for help with food and fuel, but as often as she called for herself, she called for someone else—her disabled brother, her mother- and father-in-law, her grown kids, her friends. I knew she had struggled through rehab into recovery, and through chemotherapy into remission, but I didn't know that her struggles had ended so soon. As desperate as her situation was, she always looked out for her family and friends with a fierce determination and persistence. She was a grievous angel of hardship in far Downeast Maine.

Why do people stay in Washington County? Not an easy question to answer. Certainly, some stay because they lack the ambition or the resources even to move out. Many more stay because of family ties, ancestral history, a wide freedom to live your life, good fishing and hunting, and for just the sheer raw beauty of it.

It is very hard to describe this land of high tides and leaping whales, of shattered rocks and ripping currents, of eagles and herons, to someone who hasn't seen it. It

Musicians play in front of the Tides Institute in downtown Eastport. LESLIE BOWMAN

That same self-sufficiency and independence shows itself when neighbor helps neighbor. It may be the coffee can on the checkout counter to help someone with medical bills, or the benefit supper to help the family whose house burned down, or the food pantries, yard sales, flea markets, or deer meat that is brought to someone who can't hunt anymore. Compassion and hope are not dead. If anything, they burn brighter through hardship.

• • •

Comedians may wisecrack, but it is no joke when years of poverty from a collapsed economy bring high rates of domestic violence, suicide, and petty crime, along with despair and hopelessness and self-medication with alcohol and drugs to ease the pain. Drug use in Washington County has moved with terrifying speed, from the abuse of prescription opiates like OxyContin to the real thing: heroin. Most of us know the story. State funds for addiction treatment are drying up, and law enforcement is stretched to the limit, particularly here, where a small population is spread over a vast region, much of it in unincorporated areas and tiny towns without any police force. The county sheriff has only eight deputies patrolling an area half the size of Massachusetts.

I have a theory that Washington County may be a harbinger of all of postapocalyptic America. It has been overlogged, overfished, overworked, and overlooked. The former bounty of its rivers and forests and sea have been taken and hauled away to somewhere else; it has been exploited and left drained and depleted, like a lot of other places in our great country. But it will not roll over and die.

Something new and startling has been happening here in this beleaguered region. After a number of false starts and dashed hopes over the years, Eastport is now a dozen years into a remarkable rebirth which may provide a model for other forlorn and forgotten places.

At its lowest, Eastport still had some resources: cheap real estate, a slower pace, soothing quiet, and breathtaking beauty, to mention a few. As all the other available coastal property was being bought up from Kittery to Machias, this area still had affordable old homes and saltwater farms, and people from elsewhere took notice.

Old houses have been renovated, vacant buildings have been filled, and Eastport is busier than it has been in 50 or 60 years. On any good day, the sound of hammers and saws echoes around the island, and trucks from the lumberyards rumble up and down the streets, delivering materials.

The exodus of young people has not stopped, but it is increasingly being matched by the influx of older people from away—lupine lovers. Many of these people have fled other parts of Maine, and the country, to find a slower,

becomes a part of you, and you become a part of it. Elsewhere, humankind has some semblance of control; here, nature still has the upper hand.

A living embodiment of that was "Junior," who made his living on the clam flats year-round. The first time I met him he was coming up from the shore near our camp in his clean, but old, Toyota Tercel, with some cement blocks in the back to give it traction, and several hods of squeaking clams.

"I've been to the city, but I came right back. I wouldn't trade this for anything," he said, with a sweeping gesture of his arm toward the bay. "I'm my own boss, and I can pretty much do what I want to do." What he wanted to do was earn enough to make a living and send his children to college, and to be outside winter, spring, summer, and fall. And that is just what he did.

more human-friendly pace of life. People come from other places to be renewed. Many also bring talent and experience that can enrich the life of a community. Quaint and quirky shops open, galleries spring up, music and drama find a stage on which to appear.

On the back roads, farmers and market gardeners take hold, producing local food. Where before there was only despair and depression, now there are glimmers of hope. Maybe the apocalypse was not the end of the world. Maybe what we are seeing in Washington County is a contrast to the morbid Mad Max vision of postapocalyptic America: that is, a slow, gradual healing.

• • •

You could call this the Lupine Revolution, and it is happening all over Maine, but most dramatically in some of its hardest-hit towns. It is significant that the lupine is the totemic flower of Maine, especially since it is classified as an invasive species. Lupine is attracted to what botanists call "disturbed soils." As an example, the lower fields on Blue Hill Mountain had been burned and sprayed with herbicides for commercial blueberry operations for many years, until the mid-1990s. All that grew there were blueberries; the herbicides had killed everything else.

The fields were eroded and rutted, the soil, depleted. When the land was put under conservation, the spraying stopped, and pretty soon the lupine took hold. For several years, the worn-out fields were blanketed with purple. People flocked to see the lupine, they took pictures, had picnics, weddings, and festivals.

Lupine is a legume which puts down a tough and deep root system with the ability to fix nitrogen in the soil where it grows. A stand of lupine moving into a field of worn-out soil will soon improve it so that other plants can move in too, both native and nonnative. After a few years, something strange happens: The lupine begins to shrink back to a few smaller patches while the native flora fills in and takes over. After a time a healthy, diverse flora and fauna are once more established and flourishing.

This is what the Lupine Revolution is doing in so many of our small coastal towns: rebuilding the soil, and the soul, of easternmost Maine. ♦

Rob McCall lives on Moose Island. His latest book is Great Speckled Bird: Confessions of a Village Preacher, *available from your local bookstore or W. W. Norton.*

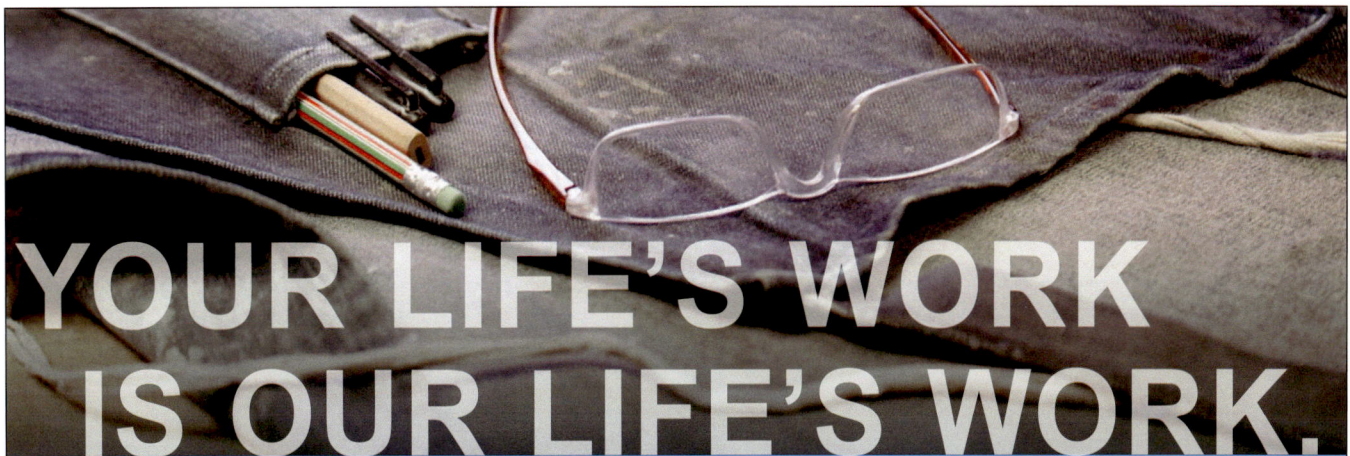

ISLAND INSTITUTE

STRENGTHENING COMMUNITY ECONOMIES

FINANCIAL & TECHNICAL SUPPORT FOR COASTAL ENTREPRENEURS

With dedicated funds and staff, we support leaders and entrepreneurs as they create visions for strong community economies, develop coastal businesses, and access the growing network of economic development resources in Maine.

The Island and Coastal Innovation Fund

is now in its sixth year. We have made eight loans and three equity investments, and have helped over 20 businesses through ICIF business support services. We will continue to invest in community-driven businesses.

140 island and coastal entrepreneurs received individualized technical assistance and/or mentoring support in the past year.

180 entrepreneurs engaged in formal group workshops and trainings designed to inspire and support business plan development.

Most Maine islands have Internet speeds about **70% slower than the national average** — barely faster than dial-up.

BETTER BROADBAND FOR MAINE'S ISLANDS AND COAST

We constantly hear islanders' concerns that the lack of reliable, high-speed broadband is a major hindrance to economic development, stability, and growth within their communities. In response, we commissioned Tilson Technology to gather more information about current broadband capacity on 13 islands and identify options on how best to improve speeds. Our goal is to help Maine's island and coastal communities gain access to reliable, high-speed broadband.

Archipelago
THE ISLAND INSTITUTE STORE

One of our first economic development programs — Since opening as Archipelago in 2000, we've supported the work of more than 840 Maine artisans.

SINCE 2000	IN 2015
$2 Million income to all Maine artists through sales revenue	**$500,000+** Sales in Rockland and online
$1 Million income to island artists	**60%** Portion of sales income returned to Maine artists

ENHANCING THE WORKFORCE & LEADERSHIP FOR THE FUTURE

AQUACULTURE IN THE CLASSROOM

Diversifying the local fishing economy is a critical need in many island communities — and the people who will power that future economy are in island and coastal classrooms today.

That's why our education team is partnering with Hurricane Island Foundation, Herring Gut Learning Center, and Casco Bay Estuary Partnership to develop an aquaculture curriculum with educators in Casco Bay and St. George. Students will develop financial literacy skills and explore aquaculture as a viable option for working on the water.

SHARING SOLUTIONS TO COMMON CHALLENGES

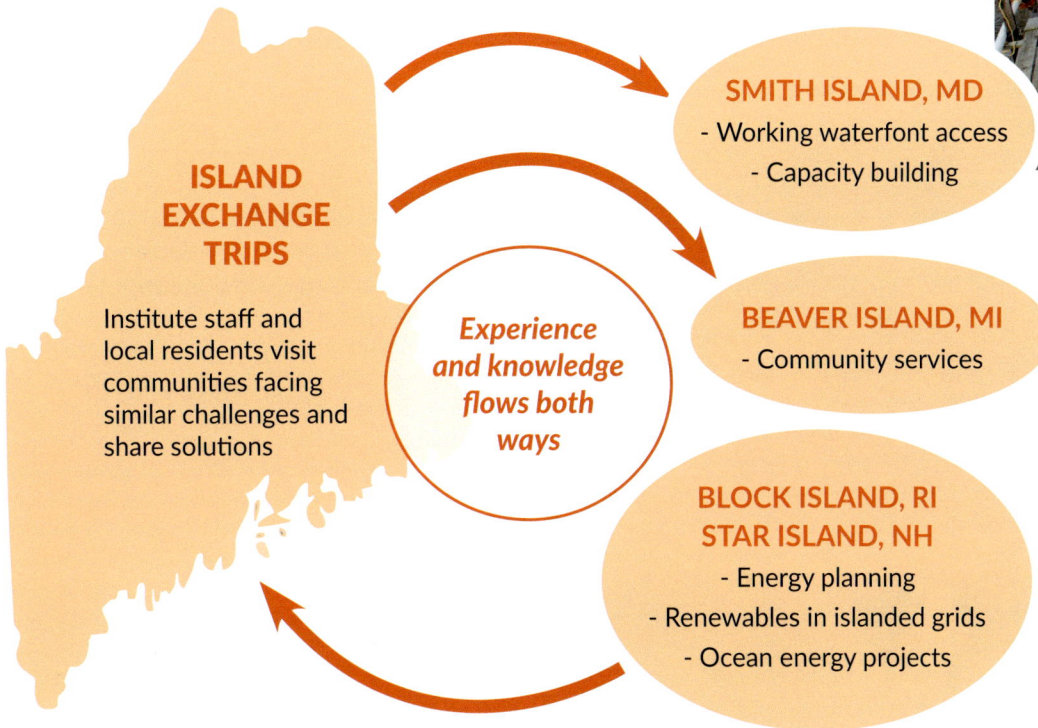

ISLAND EXCHANGE TRIPS

Institute staff and local residents visit communities facing similar challenges and share solutions

Experience and knowledge flows both ways

SMITH ISLAND, MD
- Working waterfont access
- Capacity building

BEAVER ISLAND, MI
- Community services

BLOCK ISLAND, RI STAR ISLAND, NH
- Energy planning
- Renewables in islanded grids
- Ocean energy projects

"You demonstrated an extraordinary knowledge of your islands' need and the programs which have been put in place to address them. If we can get the Great Lakes islands together, as you have done in Maine, we have an enormous opportunity."

- Peter Igoe, Beaver Island Association Board of Directors

Islands in Time Society
Gift Planning at the Island Institute

Members of the Islands in Time Society are committed to making a difference in Maine's year-round island and remote coastal communities for generations to come. Through thoughtful planning and designation of bequests, trusts, annuities, and life insurance, members craft gifts of lasting significance.

We invite you to join, and we thank our members who have chosen to make a remarkable investment in our work.

To learn more about the benefits of gift planning, contact Michelle Tussing, Vice President of Development, at mtussing@islandinstitute.org or (207) 594-9209 ext. 138.

Members

Charles Beran
John and Mary Alice Bird
Nancy McLeod Carter
Margery S. Foster
Rosalind S. Holt
Ellen V. Howe
Theodore C. Johanson
Philip and Ann Lape
Virginia B. Lloyd
Emily Lansingh Muir
Elizabeth B. Noyce
Anne P. Owsley
Molly Potter Scheu
George and Anna Shaw
Margaret L. Snow
Richard Stephenson
John and Martha Stewart
Willoughby T. Stuart
Charles O. Verrill, Jr.
H. Jeremy Wintersteen
Frances B. Youngblood

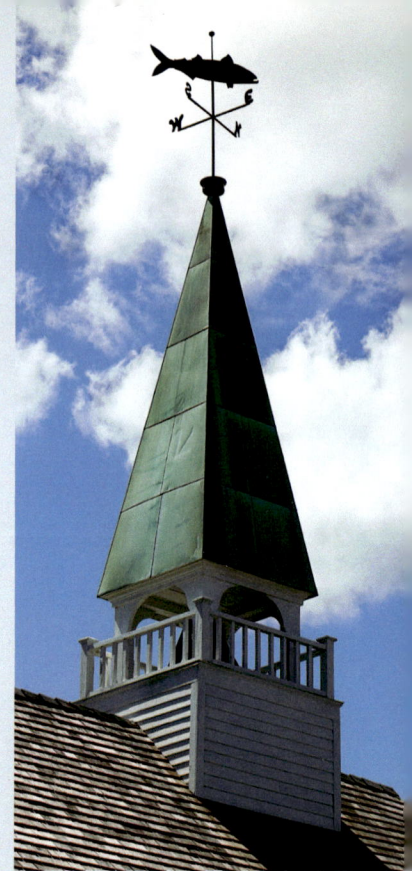

Thank you to all who have contributed to and supported the *Island Journal*, especially **Sally Engelhard Pingree** and the **Charles Engelhard Foundation**.

We believe in them.

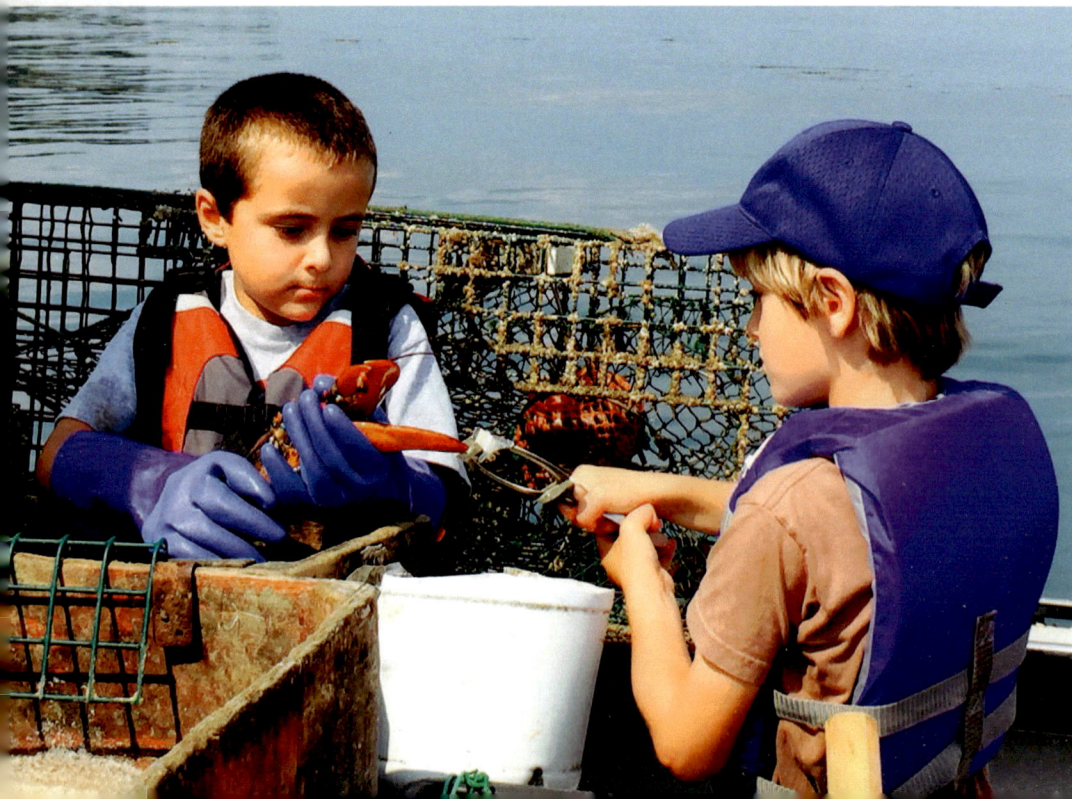

At the **Island Institute**, we see great potential in the people of Maine's islands and coast.

Join us in creating opportunities through education, leadership, business development, and more. Your support invests in the people who will help our communities thrive—now, and for years to come.

ISLAND INSTITUTE

Join us onine at:
islandinstitute.org/membership